J. F Simmons

Rural lyrics, Elegies, and Other Short Poems

J. F Simmons

Rural lyrics, Elegies, and Other Short Poems

ISBN/EAN: 9783744781480

Printed in Europe, USA, Canada, Australia, Japan

Cover: Foto ©Thomas Meinert / pixelio.de

More available books at **www.hansebooks.com**

RURAL LYRICS,

ELEGIES,

AND OTHER SHORT POEMS.

BY

HON. J. F. SIMMONS.

PHILADELPHIA:
J. B. LIPPINCOTT & CO.
1885.

Copyright, 1884, by J. B. LIPPINCOTT & Co.

TO

MISS OLIVIA P. HILL,

OF MEMPHIS, TENN.,

A FAIR, BRIGHT DAUGHTER OF THE MUSES,

THIS

LITTLE VOLUME IS DEDICATED,

AS A

MARK OF THE RESPECT AND ESTEEM ENTERTAINED
FOR HER PARENTS AND HERSELF BY

THE AUTHOR.

OH! STRIKE AGAIN THY HARP AND SING.

DEDICATION LINES.

FAIR daughter of the Muses, I
  In thy soft song have read thy soul,
And often I have wondered why
  Thou dost not seek the Poet's goal.
'Tis yonder, on the dizzy height
  Of fair Parnassus' southern peak,
Where Muses kindled first their light,
  And vot'ries taught, for gems to seek;
'Tis where—although the snows are near—
  Sweet flowers, all perennial, bloom,
And sunlight sparkles bright and clear,
  Dispersing every shade of gloom;
'Tis where the Delphian temple stands,
  And where the sweet Castalian fount
The soul of poesy expands,—
  'Tis *there* that Poets strive to mount.

Why art thou thus content below
  To dwell, thy tuneful harp unstrung?
Why Poet's sweetest dreams forego,
  And leave so much of soul unsung?
Hast thou no bright, alluring dream?
  No aspiration grand and high?
Nor yet ambition to redeem
  Souls here that in corruption lie?
Hast thou no wish to write thy name
  Up yonder, where 'twill live for aye,
Upon the pinnacle of fame,
  Which time can never wear away?

Reflect on pleasures thou canst give
　Wherever charm of song is known,
And think how selfish 'tis to live
　In aimless ease, for self alone.

Oh! strike again thy harp and sing.
　That harp no more should silent lie;
Its notes should softly, sweetly ring
　On every zephyr floating by,
Cheer drooping hearts and buoy them up,
　Sweet draughts from life's pure fountain give,
The sinking soul, bereft of hope,
　Revive, and bid it rise and live;
Do this and these, and thou shalt feel
　Thy "talent," loaned from heaven's store,
Is well employed for others' weal,
　And for thy Saviour's honor more;
And when the work of life shall close,
　Which is but scarcely now begun,
These words shall sweeten thy repose,
　For God will utter them—" Well done."

PREFACE.

THIS volume is simply what it purports to be,—a collection of lyrics and short poems, written amid the exacting duties of a busy editorial life of two or three years past. I have no apology to offer for it, and nothing to ask of critics, save fair and just treatment. It was my intention to have completed one or two narrative poems, but other duties, and lack of time, forbade my doing so.

J. F. S.

COZY NOOK, HENDERSON, KY., Dec. 1, 1884.

CONTENTS.

	PAGE
The Press	11
Rest	17
My Cousin Fannie	18
Midnight Reflections	20
Friends	22
What shall I Wear?	24
Just Beyond the Shining River	28
Wandering Thoughts	29
If?	31
Star of my Life! to Thee I Turn	33
Fare Thee Well	34
I Think of Thee	37
Ever of Thee	38
A Retrospection	40
Mary Jane	42
My Heart will Ne'er Grow Old	45
Will Spring-Time Come Again?	47
Night on the Ohio	48
The Poor Man's Friend	50
Farewell	52
"The Days that are no More"	53
Evelyn	55
Plaint of the Wounded Heart	56
Oh, would that We had Never Met!	57
A Plaited Tress	60
"Fernwood"	61
An Epitaph	65
The Serpent	66

	PAGE
Mamie's Rock	68
Thou wilt Remember	73
'Twas all a Dream	75
"The Days that are no More"	78
A Reflection	80
Whatever is is Best	82
"Jesus Wept"	84
Found! Lost!	85
Little Hetty	87
Women's Vows	88
The Dignity of Labor	90
One by One	94
Shadow and Sunshine	96
The Beautiful South	98
The Farmer's Corn and Mine	99
A Vision	100
I Know Not Why	102
The Undecorated Graves	104
To Ruth	106
"Some Time"	109
Gone to that Fair Land	111
Brown Eyes	113
Will She, too, Change?	116
"Mousey"	118
Lena Lee	120
My Birdie has Flown	122
'Tis but a Faded Flower	124
On a Picture	125
Little Pauline	126
The Flood	129
Epistle to a Young Friend	131
No Heart Concealments	135
My Life is like an April Sky	137
The Banker's Boy	139
Alas! too Late!	141
"Oh, Ever Thus!"	144
To Little Gretchen	145
First Snow	147

CONTENTS.

	PAGE
Dreams will Vanish ! Hopes will Perish	149
The Snow and the Children	151
A Child's Picture	153
Do I Love Solitude?	155
Lorena in Tears	157
My Mousey Visitor	158
The Beautiful Trio	160
Poetry	162
Parted	165
Oh, Yes, I'm Jolly (?)	167
Life's Show	170
"Your True Friend"	172
Take Back those Words	174
To my Wife	177
The Three Graces	182
Fickle Friends	183
Elmwood	185
Blind	187
A Friend's a Friend for a' That	190
When I am Gone	192
Epithalamium	194
The Stricken Heart	195
The Poet	196
Vespers (St. Peter's, Memphis)	199
Oh ! Ask Me not to Sing To-Night	200
You Sang "that Song" for Me To-Night	201
Drop by Drop	203
"Dum Spiro, Spero"	204
"Do Cotton Pay?"	206
Cantatrix Dulcissima	213
Honor	214
"Homeward now the Swallows Fly"	215
She's Sweetest when she Smiles	218
Those Eyes of Heavenly Blue	219
Birth of a Flower	221
Home	224
Around the Hearthstone	226
Song	228

RURAL LYRICS.

THE PRESS.

Written in compliance with a resolution of the Mississippi Press Association, and read before the Convention at Aberdeen, by Miss Mollie C. Duval, on Wednesday evening, June 1, 1881.

WHEN mind—the mighty pow'r which, under God,
The world commands, and rules with unwrit' code—
Looked out upon its fields of conquest vast,
And knew its future must eclipse its past,
It saw ev'n nature bow at its command,
Its creatures rode the sea and ruled the land,
Its softest song could move the hardest heart,
Its gentlest word could cause sweet tears to start,
Its touch could rough and rugged places smooth,
Its healing balms could deepest sorrows soothe,
Its magic wand could space annihilate,
Its agencies the ills of life abate,
Its eye could read the stars that decked the sky,
Its strength control the winds that whistled by,
Its skill could utilize the smallest flow'r,
And beast and savage trembled at its pow'r,

It guided fiery bolts from heaven hurled,
And governed states and nations and the world.
    And yet, although creation stood in awe,—
    Was spell-bound by the mighty works it saw,—
    One want, one need, still heavy weighed on mind:
    It nowhere in its broad domain could find
    The means at hand by which to propagate
    The truths of wisdom 'twould perpetuate.

Engraven tablets here and there were seen,
But even these were " few and far between,"
And, though the marks of wisdom's hand they bore,
'Twas not enough, for mind demanded more,—
Demanded THAT by which it might convey
Its wisdom to the peoples far away;
Some potent messenger which might extend
Its light through all the world from end to end,
Hand down its well-wrought truths from saint and sage
To unborn millions and to every age;
Demanded this, yet for it vainly sought,
For science ne'er the instrument had wrought,
Nor genius had the hidden problem solved,
Which mind had long, in faith and hope, revolved,
Its demiurgic powers kept alive,
Resolved that never it would cease to strive
Until the great, grand instrument was made
To meet a need of wisdom, truth, and trade.
Thus mind itself determined to achieve
That which should hence a crying want relieve;
It summoned all its pow'rs with stubborn will,
Its energies, its genius, and its skill,—

Invoking heaven's smiles its work to bless,
It wrought, and lo! the world received THE PRESS.
And thus, in mind of puny man, had birth
That which is now the ruling pow'r of earth;
That which, although from mortal source it came,
Has made immortal many an honored name;
Has filled the world with knowledge, truth, and light,
O'ercome oppression and supported right;
Has sown the seeds of wisdom far and wide,
Has vice condemned and all uncomely pride;
Has fostered virtue, reared her temple high,
And wielded pow'r mankind to edify.

But ev'n the rill that softest, sweetest flows,
Anon some dark, some uncouth object shows,
And from the cup which seems to foam with bliss
Will sometimes come the loathsome serpent's hiss;
The purest, warmest heart anon grows cold,
And rude alloy attaints the finest gold;
Fair Eden—home of all the pure and true—
Once, long ago, a demon's presence knew;
What, then, if here and there we sometimes find
A blur or blemish darkening the mind,
A curse on what was made alone to bless,
An evil power wielded by THE PRESS?
In search of nature's gems, we turn our eyes
Aloft, and scan the soft, cerulean skies,
And, even there, the tutored eye can trace
Uncomely spots upon the sun's bright face;

And yet the sun, all gloriously bright,
Illuminates the world with dimless light,
Sends down his rays with vivifying pow'r,
Imparting life to tree and plant and flower;
Throws out his beams on meadow, hill, and field,
And earth persuades her bounteous fruits to yield.
    The blurs are there, like spots from inky night,
    But impotent are they to dim its light,
    And, ev'n though augurs say they threatened ill,
    They only make the sun shine brighter still,—
    Enhance its virtuous power the world to bless;
    And so it is with mind's great force,—The Press.
    Excrescences have now and then appeared,
    But these, when analyzed, were never feared;
    The SOUL its unmarred purity retained,
    And life and strength and vigor still remained:
    The body still could wield resistless might
    To vanquish error and establish right.

The Press, the mighty Press, though grand and great,
Dominion wielding over man and state,
Can yet the weary hours of life beguile,
On sports of innocence serenely smile,
More brightness give to scenes that cheer the heart,
And relish to the duller ones impart;
Be harsh to vice, yet be to virtue mild,
And, like the king who gambolled with his child,
Adapt itself to every age and phase,
And ever wield resistless pow'r to please;
And many a love-lorn swain has, trembling, hung
In dread suspense for want of ready tongue,

And many a blushing maid, with equal dread,
Has watched and waited—bowed her lovely head—
Expectant, he the awful pause would break,
And while she hoped, yet feared, to hear him speak.
And there they sat, while perspiration flowed,
And each a hope and apprehension showed,
Both seeming like—so far as words and acts—
Artemas Ward's immortal forms of wax.
And who shall say how long this might have been
Had not some kindly sprite, in pity, seen
Their dread dilemma and their troubled looks,
And, in a friendly way, suggested " books!"
 The clouds dispersed! the sun shone forth to bless,
 And love received assistance from The Press!

How many a young and unfledged Cic'ro has
Pumped all in vain, and still pumped on for gas;
How many a tyro preacher, called to preach,
Has lost his ideas and his powers of speech;
How many a lawyer, 'spite of knowing looks,
Would be a clown without the printed books;
How many a doctor could have rolled his pills,
Or difference known 'twixt ipecac and squills;
How many a merchant—other business men—
Had e'er the balances on ledgers seen;
And you! ye noble men, who scissors use,—
Lest pen and ink you might, perchance, abuse,—
What hosts of you, ye editorial gang,
Have known your ideas like dark lanterns hang;
How many a one has scratched his noble head—
In search of something no one else has said,—

Has scratched it bald, and scratched it all in vain,
Alone to scratch for something there again,
    Till came the thought, but not with lightning speed,
    That books and journals might supply the need!

The world, indeed, had been a wilderness—
Ev'n with fair woman—had we not The Press.
    Wherever sun has shone, or man has dwelt,
    Or woman smiled, its power HAS been felt;
    That pow'r increases as Time's wheels roll on,
    And WILL increase until old Time is gone;
    And it should be our pride to glorify
    The talisman, and raise its standard high;
    Nay, more than talisman, for all confess
    The living pow'r and grandeur of The Press,—
    Its pow'r to spread a steady, glowing light,
    And make the darkest spots on earth grow bright;
    Its pow'r to bless mankind and elevate
    The characters alike of man and state;
    The hardest natures pliant make and soft,
    Curb dark corruption, virtue rear aloft,
    Promulgate laws by God himself sent down,
    The cross make light by showing us the crown;
    And when we contemplate its pow'rs to bless,
    Our hearts cry, *Vive le! vive le!* grand old Press!

REST.

A REST for the body and rest for the mind;
  I seek it, if but for a day,
Where hearty, affectionate welcome I'll find
  'Mong loving ones far, far away.
I've toiled without rest through the long winter nights,
  And through all the spring that has gone,
A stranger to home and its charming delights,
  A sad, silent hermit, alone.

I meet with the emblems of joy here and there,
  Yet envy not those who are blest;
I covet alone from my burden of care,
  And labor, a season of rest;
A respite which, even though however brief,
  Will bring me, at least for the while,
For overtaxed mind a much-needed relief;
  'Twill be like an angelic smile.

Worn down, I have labored and still labored on,
  And striven contented to be;
Have watched fleeting moments, and when they were
    gone,
  Looked vainly some promise to see;

Some promise of that which I needed the most,
    And yet which I never could find,
Which gladly I'd purchase at whatever cost,
    A sweet, placid rest for the mind.

But even the mind, though it be overworn,
    Exactions of duty might meet,
Its labors be done and its burdens be borne,
    And all be made pleasant and sweet,
If once and anon but a fond, loving smile
    Beamed on me to lighten each task,
And solitude's deep, gloomy dulness beguile,
    Nor would I more stimulant ask.

Here I am sitting, and wherever I look
    Mementoes past pleasure recalls,
And these are the sunrays that brighten my "Nook,"
    The pictures that hang on the walls.
I'll leave them to-morrow, and hope I shall find
    That which will be better than art,
A much-needed rest for the body and mind,
    And comfort and joy for the heart.

MY COUSIN FANNIE.

I have a fair young cousin,
    And she's happy as the bird,
Whose notes, this morning, trilling,
    From yon cedar's crest I heard.

And well she may be joyous,
    For her sky is clear and bright,
And not a shadow rises
    To obscure its cheering light.

One evening in September
    She became a blushing bride,
All her heart and soul confiding
    To the loved one at her side;
The one her heart had chosen,
    With a woman's love and faith;
And now the words were spoken
    Which united them till death.

They then began life's journey,
    In its smiling, rosy morn,
Sweet flowers blooming 'round them,
    All their pathway to adorn;
No cloud appeared above them,
    Not a thorn along their way,
But all was bright with promise
    On that happy bridal day.

As thus they sweetly started,—
    Noble husband, gentle wife,—
May their hearts be linked together
    All adown the stream of life!
And as they downward gently
    To the distant harbor glide,
Still may they journey ever
    As they started, side by side!

May dark misfortune never
 O'er their hearts a shadow fling!
May time a mellow'd pleasure
 And a sweet contentment bring!
And when life's dream is ending,
 May its closing scene be fair,
To light their way to heaven,
 And a home eternal there!

MIDNIGHT REFLECTIONS.

The mantle of night overspreads the broad sky,
 And silence is reigning supreme,
Not a thing to disturb me is hovering nigh,—
 All nature seems wrapt in a dream;
And memory's glance I instinctively cast,
 With many a wistful regret,
Along the broad vista through which I have passed,
 To scenes I can never forget.

The bright, sunny days of my life's flow'ry spring
 Come back in their freshness to view;
I cull the sweet blossoms and hear the birds sing,
 As erst I delighted to do;
I see the same sunlight as brilliantly shine,
 Hear voices I've oft heard before,
Look into soft eyes that once looked into mine,
 But ne'er will look into them more.

I think of lost friendships and ties that were sweet,
    And here and there, sometimes, a friend
In memory's vista I silently meet
    Who unfailing was to the end.
With heart heavy laden I pause now a while,
    And sigh when reflecting how few
Exemption can claim from deception and guile,
    And prove themselves constant and true.

I watch the bright sunbeams that sportively play
    Along the broad path that I came;
They linger a moment and then flit away,
    Like many a friend I could name.
I watch them in silence until they depart,
    And then seems a dark, gloomy pall
O'er the erewhile bright prospect and over my heart,
    Like a foreboding shadow to fall.

I feel that the shadow is dark'ning my brow,
    Its gloom is oppressing my heart,
And ask myself, sadly, Which of my friends now
    Will be the next one to depart?—
I mean not in death, for, although now is small
    The number I thought was a host,
I'd rather weep tears o'er the graves of them all
    Than over one living and lost.

The pains and the pleasures life's duties involve
    Come often and go with a breath.
Ah! life is a mystery no one can solve;
    'Tis solvable only by death;

And when that shall claim me perhaps I shall know,
    What now is as painful as strange,
Why friends whom I cherish too frequently show
    That they are but creatures of change.

The chimes of the town-clock have stricken the hour
    That phantoms earth's dark valleys roam,
And wield a depressing, an unrestrained pow'r,
    That wraps every object in gloom;
But yonder, above me, is gleaming afar,
    To smile on me when I look up,
A cheering, gloom-conquering, beautiful star,—
    Its name (inspiration) is *Hope!*

FRIENDS.

TO A YOUNG LADY FRIEND.

The skies are fair and clear to-night,
    The calm, sweet moon is smiling there,
And flinging down her mellow light,
    While softly floats the balmy air;
And, as I gaze on yonder skies,
    The dimless stars which there I see
Recall to mind thy soft, bright eyes,
    And waken thoughts, fair friend, of thee.

Ah! friendship is indeed a boon,—
    I do not mean the empty name,
But that which, like yon lovely moon,
    Glows ever with a steady flame;

A pure emotion, not a mood,—
 A feeling foes can ne'er estrange,
A love that no vicissitude
 Of life, nor death itself, can change.

A friendship such as this, fair one,
 A boon would be above all price,
And more than rays of summer's sun,
 Would warm and melt a heart of ice,
Would banish clouds from gloomy skies,
 A solace be for every woe,
Would gladden hearts and brighten eyes,
 And constant peace and joy bestow.

But ah! how very few indeed
 Are not by trifling cause estranged!
How fewer still, in time of need,
 Are steadfast, and remain unchanged!
How few that bear the test of time,
 Repel misfortune's sternest power,
And with a constancy sublime,
 Are truest in the darkest hour!

May all thy friends (one shall I be?),
 Like yonder stars I see above,
Be changeless, steadfast, true to thee,
 And sweeten all thy life with love.
Be true thyself, scorn every art,
 And let thy soul ne'er stoop to guile,
And may kind Heaven fill thy heart
 With joys, and ever on thee smile.

WHAT SHALL I WEAR?

The gay Widow Tompkins—as fair as a pearl—
Sat silent and pensive, her mind in a whirl,
Had pondered and pondered, and still pondered on,
Yet came no relief, nor did light seem to dawn.
She glanced in the glass, and encountered a smile,—
'Twas "chock full" of sweetness and "chock full" of
  guile,—
Her eyes were as charmingly, splendidly bright
As stars that glance down from the heavens at night;
Her neck rivalled swan's, and was white as the snow,
And each cheek wore on it a soft, rosy glow;
Her fair brow (save only when o'er it she hangs
A nondescript "thing-um-a-bob" people call bangs),
As lovely a feature as eye would behold,
O'erhung with soft tresses all silken and gold;
She seemed a bright houri, or—minus the wings—
An angel,—for she hadn't put on all her "things;"
And *there* lay the trouble, her mind was oppressed
To know how, this evening, she ought to be dressed.
A ball was at hand, and awaiting below,
Rigged nearly to death, sat an impatient beau,
Just one of that kind who are always on hand
Wheth'r coquettish maiden or widow command.
On him Widow Tompkins ne'er wasted a sigh,
Yet "used him" whenever no better was nigh,
But "oth'r fish" had she on this evening "to fry."

Her heart was as full of a scheme as her head
To make a *coup d'état;* and " thusly" she said:
" Both grave Mr. Black and gay Bendow 'll be there,
And one I must capture, now what shall I wear?
A smile is all-potent to make men my slaves;
I'll put on my sweetest and wear my new waves.
Then comes the question, Will my white satin dress,
Trimmed with point d'Alençon, or that with Duchess,
Be best my complexion and figure to show,
Win grave Mr. Black or gay Mr. Bendow?
The others may go, but I'm anxious to please—
And *do* it I must—one or t' other of these;
Much more important than 'to be or not be'
Is settling of this simple question to me.

" There's my velvet, my satins, my silks, my brocade,—
And each as becoming to a widow as maid,—
And then, there's my nun's veiling, my sweet merveillieu,
My satin De Lyon of loveliest blue,
My tarlatan, my bunting, my organdy—pink,—
But neither sets me off to advantage, I think;
There's my lovely blue silk with my white polonaise,
That seems to me ought to set men's hearts all ablaze;
And then, there's my sweet velvet, which, though very plain,
Would honor an empress, with its long flowing train;
My beautiful blue satin made *à la Princess,*
Which General Brown says is my handsomest dress;
Then my black velvet bodice, with flowing white skirt,
Whose plain, lovely neatness none would dare controvert!

Now what,—tell me, fairies,—oh! what shall I wear
To catch Black or Bendow, for they both will be there?"

Then she spread out her silks, scanned the white, pink, and blue,
The heliotrope, crimson, and the lovely écrue,
The old gold, cream, and pearl, the refreshing Nile green,
But she found fault with each, though 'twas fit for a queen;
Then the satins and velvets were brought out to view,
But all these to the wardrobe went back again, too,
And she studied and pondered and looked in the glass,
Yet could not determine what to put on, alas!
And she fast was concluding—in bitter despair—
That like one Miss McFlimsey, of Madison Square,
She, the poor Widow Tompkins, had "nothing to wear."

The clock on the mantel still resounded "tick, tick,"—
Time moved onward, and left her unable to pick;
Two dozen of dresses, and the most of them new,
Had all been rejected, for that not one would do;
And she thought and conjectured and rummaged her brain
What dress she should put on, but, alas, all in vain!
Till the clock on the mantel struck the hour to go,
While alone in the parlor awaited her beau.
Then she got out of patience, and, purely in spite,
Arrayed herself tastefully in plain, snowy white.

So she went to the party almost in despair;
She knew Mr. Black and Mr. Bendow'd be there,
And her heart was all set upon making a catch,
For with one of these she'd determined to match;
Not a moment the gay widow seemed once to suppose
The trouble with her was, she had too many clothes.
When she got to the ball she was looking so sweet
That the grave and gay widowers were soon at her feet;
She had gone out of humor,—and shall I say wroth?—
But her charms soon attracted and conquered them both.

She danced first with one and then the other a while,
First sweetly on Bendow, then on Black would she smile;
Her heart like a pendulum vibrated 'twixt two,
And to save her dear soul she knew not what to do;
Yet, around in the waltz and the " racquet" all night
She whirled and she floated in her plain snowy white;
Neither satins nor silks nor point d'Alençon lace
Did she need once to give her perfection of grace,
But, the cold cruel bangs hid one-half her sweet face.

When she went to the ball she was nervous and sad,
When she left it for home she was joyous and glad;
When she went she was bothered to know what to wear,
When she left she had conquered and then didn't care;
Black and Bendow admired the white body and skirt,
But the world called the widow a consummate flirt;
Let it say what it chose, as she ambled away,
She was proud to believe she had " carried the day;"

She had played her hand well, having gone in "to win,"
And had captured two wid'wers with plenty of " tin ;"
So, home she went happy, and would never more care
When she went to a party which dress she should wear,
No matter who else or how many'd be there.

JUST BEYOND THE SHINING RIVER.

Just beyond the shining river,
   On the flowery plains above,
Where the ransomed hosts will ever
   Bask in Jesus' smiles and love;
Where the fragrant breezes sweeping,
   Waft perfumes where angels roam;
Where there is no sigh nor weeping,
   There is my eternal home.

Just beyond the shining river,
   Where my precious ones adore
Him who suffered to deliver
   Man from death, and life restore;
Where the Saviour, kind and loving,
   Bids the weary wanderer come
Rest from toiling and from roving,
   There is my eternal home.

Just beyond the shining river,
  Where the vaults, o'erspreading, ring
With celestial music ever,
  While their anthems angels sing;
Where three darlings wait to greet me,
  'Neath the softly shining dome,
May my other loved ones meet me,
  There in my eternal home.

WANDERING THOUGHTS.

Oh! why does gloom o'er me to-day
  Its shadow fling,
And thought go wandering away
  On saddened wing?

I see upon no face a frown,
  And all seem glad.
Yet disappointment weighs me down,
  And I am sad.

I dreamed a pleasing dream last night,
  Which promise gave
That I, when came the morning light,
  Should pleasure have;

But dreams, as I have often heard,
  Contrary go,
And I, since what has now occurred,
  Believe 'tis so.

Ah me! how my lone heart does long,
    This morn, to hear
Soft, loving words or artless song
    In accents dear!

But neither shall I hear to-day,
    Nor shall I see
The singer, who is far away,—
    Away from me.

Time's wheel moves heavily and slow,
    Nor pleasure brings,
While o'er me hang dark shadows low,
    On gloomy wings.

Avaunt! ye phantom forms, away!
    Mock not my grief;
Perhaps, perhaps another day
    Will bring relief.

But life is made, though it be brief
    And full of care,
Of disappointment, pain, and grief,
    And all must bear.

So let me patiently endure,
    E'en though I sigh;
Deliverance yet will, I am sure,
    Come by and by.

IF?

If the sweetest bird that sings,
And that soars on silken wings,
Can hear a chirp of deep distress nor give the signal
    heed;
If the highest, brightest star
That is glimmering afar
Can hide its light from those to whom it is of life the
    need;
If earth's purest and its best
Can with tender feelings jest,
And see the hearts that worship them in bitter anguish
    bleed;
   Then I can see
   How it may be
That all things are not what they seem;
   That all life's glow
   Is tinsel show,—
The "baseless fabric of a dream."

And what is life, if trusted friends
Desert us to accomplish ends
Which well they know, when all are wrought,
 Although their hearts are gratified,
 And sweet success has feasted pride,
To us with bitter pain are fraught?

Ay, what is life
But woe and strife,
If those we love and trust grow cold?
'Tis only pain,
And we would fain
That icy arms our frames enfold.

But pause, ye tortured one, awhile,
And proudly smile;
Be to thyself and honor true;
Earth never knew
A warm, true heart that had not felt
A bitter blow unkindly dealt,
And thine must feel it too.
Assert thy pride,
Thine anguish hide,
And, though all bruised and sadly torn,
Let not the hand that dealt the blow
The bitter pain it gave thee know,
To laugh at thee in scorn.

If thy pure love is made the sport
Of trusted one, do not retort,
But bow and know
That though each blow
Which here it has been thine to feel
A deep wound made,
With gleaming blade,
The hand of death all wounds will heal.

STAR OF MY LIFE! TO THEE I TURN.

STAR of my life! to thee I turn
   When all the world is dark and drear,
And saddened thoughts within me burn,
   While nothing comes my life to cheer.
I wonder why the soft, sweet ray,
   So strong to soothe and charm my heart,
Is thus so coldly hid away
   When thou and I are far apart.

I know that ray still shines aglow,
   Although its glints I may not see,
And I would give my life to know
   It only lives and beams for me.
But, then, when not a shimmer comes
   Athwart the intervening space,
I'm haunted by dark mocking gnomes,
   That chill my heart and strand its peace.

Yet from the fount of faith I drink;
   I could not doubt a soul like thine;
I'd rather welcome death than think
   That ray can for another shine;
And faith alone my heart sustains,
   While slowly drags each gloomy day,
And silence, all unbroken, reigns,
   Nor echo comes from far away.

But ah! 'tis possible, I know,
    However marvellous and strange,
That even stars which brightest glow
    May yet, in time's mutations, change.
If now, or ever, this shall be,
    Then would I, in some land afar,
Where none my bitter woe might see,
    Breathe out my life to thee, sweet star!

FARE THEE WELL.

"Fare thee well, and if forever,"
    'Tis alone by thy decree,
Yet ev'n this will fail to sever
    Ties that bind my soul to thee.
From thy side though I be banished,
    From thy heart, alas! as well,
And my sweetest hopes have vanished,
    Never can my heart rebel.

Time moves onward, bringing changes,
    Soul from soul it rifts apart,
Heart from loving heart estranges,
    Wounding as with poisoned dart;
Yet, even in the darkest hour,
    Love it never can subdue,—
This defies its utmost power
    When the heart that loves is true.

I have loved thee so sincerely
  That, although the cruel blow
Thou hast given wounds severely,
  Change my heart can never know;
All its love to thee was given,
  Thine it will through life remain,
Though I be in exile driven,
  And we never meet again.

Yet to thee will come reflection,
  Which can only bitter prove,
When comes up the recollection
  Of our fondly-plighted love;
Thou wilt think of words once spoken
  When I held thy hand in mine,
And of golden ties now broken,—
  Broken by a word of thine;

Vows of love, to be eternal,
  Which to me were draughts of bliss,
Vows of love that seemed supernal,
  Sealed with fondly-lingering kiss;
Vows which, though by thee now broken,
  Linger in thy memory yet,
And, with all the words then spoken,
  Thou, I know, canst ne'er forget.

Ah! how fondly I believed thee!
  How I trusted! how I loved!
Never varied nor deceived thee,
  But to thee unchanging proved;

Gave thee all my heart's devotion,
    Love that was almost divine,
Deep and boundless as the ocean,—
    Thine to be, and only thine.

Even when thy heart has wavered,
    And, o'ercome by artful wiles,
Others, o'er me, thou hast favored,
    On them lavishing thy smiles,
Then, when skies were darkest seeming,
    Nor a glimmer in them shone,
Trusting still, I went on dreaming,
    Dreaming of thee as my own.

Though I have for thee endeavored
    All to do that could be done,
Yet the once sweet ties are severed
    By thine own dear hand alone;
Beams no ray of light above me,
    Dark despair alone is mine,
And, though all the world should love me,
    This is nothing without thine.

Yes, farewell, and if forever,
    'Tis by thy decree alone,
Yet that mandate cannot sever
    Ties the sweetest life has known;
These will linger, ev'n when dying,
    Tongue no more my love may tell;
But, farewell! my heart is sighing
    While it whispers, "Fare thee well."

I THINK OF THEE.

I THINK of thee when in the East
　The rosy tints of morn appear,
And matin anthems—nature's feast—
　Fall sweetly, gently, on the ear;
Then all is soft and pure and fair,
　And earth is robed in purity,
And I can fancy, then and there,
　The scene is typical of thee.

I think of thee when solar beams,
　At mid-day's sultry, melting hour,
Come down in glittering, glowing streams,
　With sweeping, scorching, burning pow'r;
And then I think, as from above
　The scintillations flash and dart,
They typify the burning love
　Which thou hast kindled in my heart.

I think of thee when in the west,
　Upon his glowing, crimson bed,
The God of Day lies down to rest,
　And hides from view his golden head;
And in the soft, sweet, rosy hue
　Which tints the canopy the while,
My love transforms the charming view
　Into thy loving, blushing smile.

I think of thee when darkness reigns,
    And silence, undisturbed and deep,
The animated world enchains
    In " nature's sweet restorer,"—sleep.
I fancy then that if thy head
    Were pillowed on my loving breast,
We ne'er should storm nor sorrow dread,
    For both would be supremely blest.

Forgive the vain, ambitious thought,
    Nor one sweet word to me deny:
I know the vision hope hath wrought
    Can only languish, droop, and die;
And yet, when comes the reaper, Death,
    To lay his icy hand on me,
I'll whisper with my latest breath
    Thy name, sweet one, and think of thee.

EVER OF THEE.

Ever of thee while the starlight is streaming
    From myriads of heaven's bright lanterns above,
Though vainly, I'm tenderly, silently dreaming,
    And balming thy name in an ocean of love.

I mingle with others, and yet I feel lonely,
    For only thy presence can happiness give;
I long for thee, dearest, for thee and thee only:
    Alone in thy smile and thy love I would live.

Be clouds o'er me threat'ning, my heart filled with
    sorrow,
My cup overflowing with wormwood and gall,
When even from hope no relief I can borrow,
    One smile of thine, dearest, can dissipate all.

I love thee, I love thee, alas! love thee madly;
    I know it too well, yet the love-flame *will* burn;
'Tis sweet to my heart, though it moans, oh, so sadly!
    To think it may never be blessed with return.

And yet, dearest one, I am certain that never
    Thou'st had or canst have such devotion as mine;
I gave it thee freely, and gave it forever,
    And, though unrequited, 'twill ever be thine.

Though mine be the sorrow, think not I shall blame
    thee;
    I ever pray, dearest, that thou mayst be blest,
Shall love thee forever, and only will name thee
    As dearest and purest and sweetest and best.

And now, dearest one, must the hopes that I cherish
    No longer around thy dear image entwine?
One sweet promise whisper, and hope can ne'er perish;
    Say only, sweet darling, "Forever I'm thine."

A RETROSPECTION.

I sit me here this sultry day,
   And saddened, longing glances cast
Along the checkered, winding way—
   The vista—of the fading past.
And, as I gaze, the prospect seems
   A cheerless, sombre hue to wear,
E'en though anon the sunlight gleams,
   A fleeting moment, here and there.

Now comes to view a smiling glen,
   Within whose shades I've sought repose;
A modest lily now and then,
   And here and there a blushing rose;
I hear anon the mock-bird's song,
   The petulant and crafty jay;
I see the brooklet dance along,
   And gaze on hill-tops far away.

I see the night-shades gath'ring near,
   And gloom o'erspreads the plain and grove,
And then the moon and stars appear,
   Bright beacons in the skies above;
I feel deep shadows on my brow,
   That corresponding thoughts impart,
Like those that weigh upon me now,
   While sadness fills my aching heart.

But, as the darkness grows apace,
   I turn my eager, wistful eyes,—
As if in search of some dear face,—
   And watch the stars in yonder skies,
Until bright Venus seems to smile
   And beckon me up there to rest;
Then I forget my griefs the while,
   And feel serenely, sweetly blest.

But, ah! like sweetest dream I've known
   The vision all too soon is past;
I catch a glimpse, and it is gone:
   It was too bright, too sweet to last;
Too bright, alas! for such as I;
   It slowly vanished from my sight,
And left me all alone to sigh,
   Yet while it lasted it was bright.

Then comes a scene of long ago,
   When one I knew all free from guile
O'erwhelmed my soul with bitter woe,
   Yet banished all with one sweet smile;
This could alone my heart revive,
   Could raise my drooping spirits up,
Away all gloomy phantoms drive,
   And fill my thirsting soul with hope.

But let me look no farther now;
   Let mem'ry fondly dwell on this,
Lest clouds again o'erspread my brow
   And hide the view that brought me bliss;

The past has checkered been and rough,
   And I have longed for dreamless rest,
But one such mem'ry is enough,
   And in this one I now am blest.

MARY JANE.

Can one forget his school-boy days
   Ere earnest life begun?
His daily tasks, his noonday plays,
   His trials, and his fun?
The time he strolled, like other chaps,
   At eve, along the lane,
And said sweet things and stole, perhaps,
   A kiss from Mary Jane?

'Tis said that as man older grows
   His mental lights grow dim,
But girls, in his young days, he knows
   Were not "stuck up" nor prim;
And if "Miss Grundy" called 'em pert,
   And frivolous, and vain,
He thinks of one this did not hurt,
   And 'twas his Mary Jane.

And through the vista oft he looks
   Back to those early years,
The school-day friends, the well-thumbed books,
   And often looks through tears;

For well he knows that many a friend
  Is gone, and few remain,
And sad sweet memories often blend
  Around his Mary Jane.

Ah! I remember, long ago,
  I walked an extra mile
Each afternoon through dust or snow
  For just one parting smile;
'Twas given with a sweet " good-by,"
  Whose accents I retain
In tender memory, and sigh
  For gentle Mary Jane.

Our parting-place was near the gate,
  Upon a sloping hill,
Away back in the " Old North State,"
  Close by an ancient mill;
I've wished I could the sun command
  (But knew the wish was vain)
While there I stood and clasped the hand
  Of blushing Mary Jane.

At morn we met with loving looks,
  Infringing ne'er a rule,
And I was proud to " tote" her books
  As on we trudged to school;
I helped her if her task was hard,
  And when I made it plain,
A soft, sweet smile was my reward
  From lovely Mary Jane.

One morn I walked with eager feet,
    Joy beaming on my face,
The dear one as before to meet
    At the accustomed place;
When I was late a mark she'd make
    Upon the roadside plain,
And then I'd haste to overtake
    My gentle Mary Jane.

But on that morning, bright and fair,
    When I came near the gate,
No mark nor Mary Jane was there,
    So down I sat to wait;
But soon swept by a messenger,
    Who cried out from the lane,
" I'm going for the doctor, sir,
    To see Miss Mary Jane."

I had no heart for school that day,
    My lessons all forgot,
I tried to drive my fears away,
    But found that I could not;
My schoolmates all, as I could see,
    My teacher too, 'twas plain,
Were sad as I, for all, like me,
    Loved gentle Mary Jane.

But, ah! why now that time recall?
    It can no good betide;
Two words will tell the story, all,
    Alas! those are, " she died";

And I, when mem'ry comes, cannot,
    Ev'n now, my tears restrain,
For I have never yet forgot
    My long-lost Mary Jane.

Though other scenes have come and gone,
    And honeyed tongues beguiled,
And other fair ones have, anon,
    Upon me sweetly smiled,
Yet memory has held, and will
    Through all my life retain,
Those morns and eves upon the hill
    With dear lost Mary Jane.

MY HEART WILL NE'ER GROW OLD.

The years have swiftly flown away,
    And o'er me shadows flung,
My beard and locks are growing gray,
    But still my heart is young;
And till it shall like marble be,
    As pulseless and as cold,
Howe'er the world shall deal with me,
    It never will grow old.

Though grief has oft my bosom torn
    And bitter anguish wrung,
I bear the pain, as I have borne,
    And still my heart is young.

Though on me all the world shall frown,
    And miseries untold
Shall weigh upon and bear me down,
    My heart will ne'er grow old.

Though loved ones may no longer sing
    The songs for me they sung,
And time may o'er them changes bring,
    Yet still my heart is young.
Though time may to my anxious eye
    A future dark unfold,
And from my heart wring many a sigh,
    That heart will ne'er grow old.

Though loved and trusted ones have changed,
    And cruelly have stung,
And are from me, alas! estranged,
    My heart continues young;
And though they meet me with a glance
    Indifferent and cold,
That wounds my heart like poisoned lance,
    That heart will ne'er grow old.

And when old age my frame shall clasp,
    And palsied be my tongue,
Though I may tremble in its grasp,
    My heart will still be young;
And when death comes on me to lay
    His hand, all icy cold,
I'll know, ev'n as I pass away,
    My heart will ne'er grow old.

WILL SPRING-TIME COME AGAIN?

THE forest leaves are brown and sere,
   And, in the chilly autumn breeze,
Are blown and scattered far and near
   From off the sad and silent trees;
I see them scattered o'er the ground,
   And sad the tall oaks seem to be;
I ask myself, when looking round,
   Will spring-time come again to me?

The spring and summer both are gone,
   The roses now no longer bloom,
The vine seems desolate and lone,
   The garden wrapped in sombre gloom;
The song-birds now no longer fill
   The grove with soft, sweet melody,
And my sad heart is asking, will
   The spring-time come again to me?

How tenderly, and sadly yet,
   The eager glance of memory turns
To scenes the heart can ne'er forget!—
   The scenes for which it ever yearns!—
And willingly it would forego
   Its present dreams, whate'er they be,
Could it by intuition know
   Spring-time will come again to me.

Spring may not come to me again,
   And I, perhaps, have seen my last,
Yet saddened memory will retain,
   Till death shall come, the fadeless past;
The words which in that past I hear,
   The smiles which in that past I see,
All gone with spring, and oh! will e'er
   Sweet spring-time come again to me?

It may not come again, but I
   Can look away in hope and faith
For rest from labor by and by,
   And my sad heart will welcome death;
And if, ere winter's reign is o'er,
   Shall come its cold and stern decree,
I know that on fair Aidenn's shore
   Sweet spring will come again to me.

NIGHT ON THE OHIO.

Written on board the steamer H. T. Dexter, August, 1884.

The waters are placid, the breezes are soft,
   And oceans of brilliants are streaming
From myriads of beautiful stars up aloft,
   There calmly and silently beaming.

While sitting and gazing, I seem to have caught
   A touch of divine inspiration,
And fancy a bright, charming vision hath wrought,
   Of love's most endearing creation.

I see in the brightness of yon stars above
   Resemblance that can't be mistaken,
To bright lustrous eyes where I read worlds of love,
   And faith that can never be shaken.

I hear in the breezes a soft, soothing voice,
   That fills me with pleasing emotions,
And causes my o'erburdened heart to rejoice,
   And softens its purest devotions.

And in the reflections, that silently now
   Play sweetly upon the calm waters,
I plainly behold the resplendent fair brow
   Of one among earth's fairest daughters.

And then yonder cloud-bank that floats in the sky,
   As shapely as aught here below it,
The same peerless Houri presents to mine eye,
   The dream and the hope of the poet.

And thus in the beauties around and above,
   And those that are down on me streaming,
I see the dear image of her whom I love,
   Of whom day and night I am dreaming.

THE POOR MAN'S FRIEND.

The rich man has a host of friends,
　The poor man has but one;
The first stand firm till fortune ends,
　The last when there is none.
The first all wear transparent smiles
　Until their idols fall;
The last is free from arts and wiles,
　And never smiles at all.

The first will cluster round their man
　Like bees around a flow'r,
And, like the bees, make all they can
　In fortune's sunny hour;
But when the gloomy clouds appear,
　And dark becomes the day,
They some contagion seem to fear,
　And hasten then away.

The rich man's friends his money love,
　Enjoy his wealth with greed,
But, riches gone, they rarely prove
　His friends in time of need.
They with him drink and dine and sup,
　And watch his smile or frown;
They fawn and flatter while he's up,
　But kick him when he's down.

The poor man's friend is like the rock
    That meets the tempest blast,
And stands unmoved the rudest shock
    Till all the storm is past;
Embedded 'neath the waves aground,
    Though lightnings flash and glare,
And winds and billows beat around,
    It still stands firmly there.

The poor man's friend is free from guile,
    Nor aught can weigh him down;
He neither covets fortune's smile
    Nor dreads misfortune's frown;
The last, indeed, which men are wont
    To deem of ills the worst,
He meets with calm and careless front,
    But hides when comes the first.

And by the poor man he will stand
    The closer in distress,
Though hard and horny be his hand
    And tattered be his dress;
On sunny or on cloudy day,
    In heat or cold the same,
He's driven but by death away,
    And POVERTY's his name.

A friend indeed that shames mankind,
    Whom trifles oft estrange,
Nor can you one more steadfast find,
    Or one so free from change.

He heeds not frown, nor scorn, nor scoff,
  But clings unyielding still,
Nor can you shun or shake him off,
  Although you have the will.

Let others bend the "supple hinge"
  Of knee each day and hour,
In servile adulation cringe,
  Like slaves, to wealth and power;
False-heartedness I spurn away,
  The true alone defend,
And, in the pure, clear draught to-day,
  I toast "The Poor Man's Friend."

FAREWELL.

"Farewell, if ever fondest prayer
  For others' weal availed on high,"
Then mine will wing thy name up there,
  The burden of a saddened sigh;
'Twill plead and importune for thee,
  That peace and joy thy cup may fill,
That all thy life may happy be,
  And thus I good return for ill.

'Twere vain to cherish, now, regret,
  Since I thy fickleness have seen,
Yet thou I know canst ne'er forget
  The past through which we both have been;

But thou hast cancelled every vow,
   'Twere useless on the theme to dwell,
By thy behest we're parted now,
   And I can only say "farewell."

"THE DAYS THAT ARE NO MORE."

"Dear as remembered kisses after death,
And sweet as those by hopeless fancy feigned
On lips that are for others; deep as love,
Deep as first love, and wild with all regret;
O death in life, the days that are no more."
                  TENNYSON.

THE chilly autumn breeze goes sweeping by,
   And soon the forest-trees their leaves will cast,
And these upon the frozen ground will lie,
   To rustle in the bitter wintry blast;
The mocking-birds no more their anthems sing,
   Nor summer swallows o'er the tree-tops soar;
The russet leaves and withered herbage bring
   To memory's eye "the days that are no more."

The mind still lingers on each happy scene
   Of other days, and fancy fondly weaves
A garland, which 'twould fain keep bright and green,
   But fate has browned it like the autumn leaves;
Alas! that eyes which erst with love-light shone,
   The face that once sweet smiles of welcome wore,
Now coldly turn and leave me all alone
   With memory of "the days that are no more."

The cordial grasp, the soft and tender glance,
    The loving words that vigor gave to hope,
The sylph-like form that floated through the dance,
    To memory's view come softly looming up;
Come softly, sweetly, yet on gloomy wings,
    For all the hopes awakened then are o'er,
And tender recollection only brings
    To memory's view " the days that are no more."

Then life seemed bright, with priceless pleasures blest,
    And it was sweet to dream the hours away,
To let my soul upon hope's anchor rest,
    And dream of bliss in some near future day;
The skies that floated lightly o'er my head
    Their softest, sweetest tints of azure wore,
But now they wear a sombre hue instead,
    When memory brings " the days that are no more."

When come to mind the shattered hopes, which erst
    Could make the darkest cloud with brightness beam,
Then vanished, as the shining bubbles burst
    Upon the surface of the glassy stream,
Ah! how the saddened, stricken heart will crave
    White wings on which away from earth to soar,
Or rest to find within the dreamless grave,
    And there forget " the days that are no more."

EVELYN.*

As fair as the lily that blooms by the stream,
As placid as childhood's first innocent dream,
As gentle as lambkin that plays on the lawn,
As lovely as rose-tinted sky at the dawn,
As modest as cereus, that blossoms at night,
As pure as the moonbeams, all spotlessly bright,
A sweeter, a fairer, a lovelier flow'r
Blooms not here on earth, nor in Eden's fair bow'r.

The light of intelligence brightens her eye,
And transparent dimples her cheeks beautify,
Her features all perfect, as perfect can be,
No fair, gentle lassie more lovely than she;
Her carriage is graceful, and faultless her form,
Her heart sympathetic, and tender, and warm,
A type of the fairest of angels above,
And not one is purer, or sweeter to love.

Sweet Evelyn, thine image is now here with me,
And fondly my orison 'rises for thee,
That heaven upon thee benignantly smile,
Protect thy pure heart from distress and from guile,
Exempt the skies o'er thee from shadows and gloom,
And cause fadeless flow'rs on thy pathway to bloom,
Make all thy life joyous, and when it is past,
Then give thee a home with the angels at last.

---

* Little Evelyn Brown, daughter of the Hon. John Young Brown, of Henderson, Kentucky.

PLAINT OF THE WOUNDED HEART.

The thought of death is sweet to me;
　The prospect has alone one blot,—
It is that I, alas! shall be
　By loved ones then so soon forgot.
I know 'twill not disturb me when
　The cold, damp dew is on my brow,
For I shall be all heedless then;
　And yet it does disturb me now.

But, after all, perhaps 'twere best
　To die and be forgotten, too,
Than live in sorrow and unrest
　When hope's bright visions fade from view;
For these, though potent while they last
　To cheer the heart and calm the mind,
Leave only, when forever past,
　Deep, dark, and dismal shades behind.

For disappointment, silent grief,
　When sighs are borne on every breath,
There is, alas! but one relief,
　One panacea, and that is death;
It cures all ills, heals every pain,
　Oblivion's mantle o'er them throws;
It lulls the hopes we know are vain,
　And gives the troubled heart repose.

Oh, Saviour! hear my prayer to-night;
　　There's little joy in life for me.
I've tried so hard to live aright,
　　And ever true in heart to be,
And yet have seen the loved grow cold,
　　Which I had ne'er believed, though I
Had, by a Prophet's tongue, been told
　　That change would come and love would die.

I thought me once of earthly bliss;
　　Alas! the thought has passed away,
And left a shadow—only this,—
　　To tell me, "Fondest hopes decay."
But, Saviour, calm my troubled breast,
　　Drive back these shadows of despair;
I know in heav'n alone is rest;
　　Oh, Saviour! let me find it there!

OH, WOULD THAT WE HAD NEVER MET!

Oh, would that we had never met!
　　But, ah! the waking comes too late;
'Twas sweet to worship thee, and yet
　　Thy hand has led me to my fate.
　　　　Thy tender, loving words to me
　　　　　　Were balms to heal the deepest wound,

My trusting soul believed in thee
  It had its longed-for idol found.
It gave thee love, and faith, and all
  That idolizing soul could give,
Thou didst its very life enthrall,
  And in thy smile 'twas sweet to live.

Oh, would that we had never met!
  But thou hast spoken words to me,
Sweet words, which thou canst ne'er forget,
  Though joyous all thy life may be.
And if, perchance, in later years,
  Those memories should provoke a smile,
And never pain, regret, nor tears,
  But yield thee sport alone the while,
Yet thou wilt think amid thy fun
  How dearly I for this have paid,
Though coldly thou mayst look upon
  The wreck and ruin thou hast made.

Oh, would that we had never met!
  The skies are dark'ning o'er my head,
A storm is gath'ring o'er me, yet
  It does not waken aught of dread.
I see the wrecks around me fall,
  The storm-king seems to mock control,
And yet I calmly gaze on all,
  For anguish rages in my soul;
I sit within the tempest's path,
  And while the skies in torrents weep,
I pray the storm-king in his wrath
  May me from earth and sorrow sweep.

Oh, would that we had never met!
But, ah! the wish is worse than vain,
And vainer still is all regret,
    Though we may never meet again.
    I may, perhaps, have been to thee
        A thing of pastime,—scarcely more,—
    And thou, with friends, hath mocked at me
        As none have ever done before;
    Yet gladly I'd promote thy weal,—
        As well thou knowest I have sought,—
    And pray thy heart may never feel
        The anguish thou in mine hath wrought.

Oh, would that we had never met!
    The past can never be forgot
By either me or thee, and yet
    I blame thee not, I blame thee not.
    My soul's deep anguish I would hide
        Where it can never rise to view,
    Thy cruel fickleness to chide,
        When I have never been untrue;
    I still am true to every vow,
        And as when last we said " good-by"
    I loved thee, so I love thee now,
        And so shall love thee till I die.

A PLAITED TRESS.

On the heart whose devotion will tenderly lave it,
    Save when 'tis drawn forth but to gladden mine eyes,
On the heart where is reigning the dear one who gave it
    It softly and sweetly and lovingly lies;
On the heart which will ever and fondly adore it,
    And guarding it ever with tenderest care,
Yet longs that the beautiful head that once wore it
    Were pillowed confidingly, lovingly, there.

I draw it forth gently and look on it nightly;
    It conjures up soft, soothing visions of bliss,
And seems to smile sweetly and glisten more brightly
    Whene'er I press on it love's lingering kiss;
"With love"—so she said—unto me it was given;
    Her love is a treasure that angels might prize;
It gave me a glimpse and a foretaste of heaven
    To read it one morn in her bright, lustrous eyes.

Her own heart has told her how fondly I love her,
    That only in her loving smile would I live,
That nothing on earth could I treasure above her,
    Nor covet aught else that kind heaven could give.
The sweet words she gave me I'm sure I shall never
    Forget while remains to me lingering breath,—
Although we are parted (it may be forever),
    They'll live in my mem'ry till banished by death.

"FERNWOOD."

(Written in Fernwood Cemetery, Henderson, Kentucky.)

Afar from all the stirring scenes of life,
   Its busy mart, its eager, hurrying throng,
Its wild confusion, toil, and care, and strife,
   Its gay carousals and its ribald song;

Afar from all that might the mind disturb
   Or undue bias give to roving thought;
Afar from all that might reflection curb,
   Or dreams dispel by sober fancy wrought;

I sit me down where cooling shades invite,
   'Neath overspreading boughs in verdure clad;
The breezes play around me soft and light,
   And murmurs linger near, both sweet and sad.

I here and yon a swain and lassie see,
   In blissful heedlessness of stranger's eye,
Forgetful they, in happy, thoughtless glee,
   That hundreds here in dreamless slumber lie.

But as the rays of summer's sun recede,
   And gather slowly in the western zone,
These thoughtless ones the coming shadows heed,
   And, hieing homeward, leave me here alone.

Ah me! how like the fickle, changing world
  Of human-kind, who, when is bright the day,
Will by us stand; but night's dark pall unfurled,
  They hie themselves with eager feet away!

Could I to life bring back the sleeping dust,
  How many here could tell a tale of woe,
Of harsh unkindness, violated trust,
  Or undeserv'd and bitter, cruel blow!

Perhaps some sleeper here, in calm repose,
  Beyond the reach of turmoil, pain, and strife,
A tale of wrong and sorrow might disclose,
  Which made death's call a sweet relief from life.

Too oft the tall, imposing stones that rise
  O'er mould'ring dust and ashes little mean;
Each carving tells of him who 'neath it lies,
  "Not what he was, but what he should have been."

Anon a simple, unpretentious line
  Speaks more than volumes, yet it leaves unsaid
A thousand deeds fond mem'ries still enshrine,
  A sacred incense round the slumb'ring dead.

Here sleep the rich, the poor, the proud and great,
  The humble, undistinguished—nay, unknown—
Beside the men of fame and men of state,
  And over all alike the night-winds moan.

The honored matron who her life resigned—
  Her duties all performed—to find sweet rest,
Perhaps not thinking she would leave behind
  A countless host to rise and call her blest;

The lovely maiden, in whose sparkling eye
  Intelligence and warm affection shone;
The white-haired sire and infant scion lie
  Beneath this turf, and each one lies alone.

If all the eloquence reposing here
  Could wake again to speak in righteous cause,
The very stones, that heedless all appear,
  Would rise and voice a long and loud applause.

The time has been when list'ning Senates hung
  In rapt attention on the thrilling sounds
That fell like gems from some now silent tongue
  That stilly lies within these sacred grounds.

Yet this is called a "city of the dead,"
  Though not a sound is borne upon the air;
Perhaps the sleepers hover o'er my head,
  And hold communion with each other there.

'Tis sweet to think, when dear ones hence depart,
  That those they loved remain to them still dear,
And sweet to feel within the mourning heart
  That they to us are still and ever dear.

The partings death upon us brings would be
  Beyond the pow'r of tender hearts to bear,
Could eye of faith no longed-for haven see,
  And feel that all would be together there.

Thank God! "It is not all of life to live,"
  Else bitter wounds received would ne'er be healed,
The keenest those which hands of loved ones give,
  Their depth to be by death alone revealed.

But shades of evening, spreading o'er me fast,
  A warning give that "time is on the wing,"
And, like the summer day that now is past,
  I, too, must pass away, and everything.

The moss-stained slabs that here and yonder lie,
  The grass-grown mound, the tall, imposing stone,
All tell me men are living but to die,
  And then?—what then Omniscience knows alone.

Adieu, sweet shades! I hie me homeward now;
  The moon steals forth to scatter here her gems,
The stars look sweetly down from night's calm brow,
  And zephyrs pause to chant soft requiems.

Adieu! while homeward now I wend my way;
  Thy sacred precincts are in loving hands,
For "mounting guard" begins with parting day,
  And over all are hov'ring angel bands.

AN EPITAPH.

Angels! pure and bright and fair,
Take this dear one to thy care;
Angels! ye who dwell above,
Guard her with a deathless love;
She was here the purest, best,
Let her there be ever blest.

Angels! when the trump shall sound,
Calling from the cold, cold ground
Those who loved each other here,
Those to heart and memory dear,
Then I beg thee, angels, guide
Me to this dear loved one's side.

Here on earth, a little while,
I have lived within her smile;
Angels! now that smile is gone,
And my heart is sad and lone;
This I ask and only this,
Let me dwell with her in bliss.

THE SERPENT.

Although he crawls in stealth alone, as nature first
  decreed,
And finds congenial resting-place beneath the noxious
  weed,
And though his proper home is in the forest, dark and
  deep,
Anon he spreads his filthy slime where reptiles do not
  creep.

No home so sacred, not a tie so tender or so dear,
No circle so secluded, but whose holy atmosphere
He would with deadly poison and with slimy filth
  invade,
And rudely there his venom throw to taint its peaceful
  shade.

The great Creator of the world, when all his work was
  done,—
Man, animal, the earth, the sky, the stars, the moon,
  the sun,—
Linked then each kind together in the ties of brother-
  hood,
And looked upon his finished work and "saw that it
  was good."

He made the reptiles, and he made the slimy things to
   crawl,
Yet one of these insidiously wrought man's eternal fall,
And in that fall, the saddest thing that could have
   taken place,
Was serpent's nature then infused into the human race.

And so it was, and so it is, that far the greater harm
Has been, and is, by reptiles done, who wear the human
   form;
They taint the very air we breathe with poisoned, fetid
   breath;
Too mean and vile they are to live, and yet unfit for
   death.

Concealed behind a flimsy veil or hidden in the dark,
They aim their gross and filthy shafts at some exalted
   mark;
And always aim above themselves, as if they did not
   know
That envious and malicious shafts invariably fall low.

And those who will not tread with them the dark and
   devious path,
Are sure to meet, but rarely feel, their hell-envenomed
   wrath;
The sweetest flowers, if they can, they deal a deadly
   wound,
But all their vile and hellish shafts will now and then
   rebound.

No viler reptiles than are these on earth's broad domain
    dwell,
Nor even could their counterparts be vomited from hell,
And God Himself, who in their hearts and all their
    vileness sees,
Has made a darker, deeper hell alone for such as these.

MAMIE'S ROCK.*

AN ALLEGORY.

I stood one summer day, not long ago,
    Where maddened nature once her wrath had shown;
Perhaps her purpose was that man might know
    How vast her pow'r, which erst he had not known.

High up in mid-air stony monsters frowned,
    Their craggy fronts betok'ning hoary age,
Anon their tow'ring summits verdure crowned,
    Relieving scars and marks of tempests' rage.

---

* On a romantic little stream in Southern Illinois, among hundreds of gigantic rocks, is a beautiful flat-top stone nearly square,—a romantic trysting-place for lovers,—which bears on it in large plain letters the words "Mamie's Rock." The legend connected with it I may relate hereafter.

These frowning rocks, a giant brotherhood,
  In double file, grim-visaged, dark and still,
In awe-inspiring, silent grandeur stood,
  While 'twixt them flowed a bright meandering rill.

'Twas like sweet childhood 'mid a warlike band,—
  All pleasing one, the other all austere,
Simplicity the one, the other grand,
  The one all bright, the other dark and drear.

O'er rocky bed the sparkling waters flowed,
  Through narrow gorge, and then in broad expanse,
And as I gazed the whole broad prospect showed
  Some new sublimity at every glance.

Long years ago, perhaps ere man had trod
  With slow and measured, or with eager feet,
The rough gray stones or yielding earth which God,
  The world's great architect, had left complete,

Here nature, in creation's early morn,
  Convulsions had which shocked her own calm rest,
By which, too, these gigantic rocks were torn
  In rude upheavals from earth's trembling breast.

It may have been a "battle of the rocks,"
  While awe-struck shrubs and trees stood trembling by,
And, in their onsets and terrific shocks,
  These fragments here were scattered where they lie.

And then, unheralded by trump or fame,
   A little rill, bright, sparkling, and serene,
The combat seeing, softly, sweetly came,
   To separate the hosts, and flowed between.

It paused not till the battle-field it passed,
   The angry hosts were stilled and silence reigned,
Then it a glance of sweet contentment cast
   Back where its sweet influence had war restrained.

How like the pow'r which lovely woman wields!
   Her fickleness or frown can peace destroy,
Her gentleness and love, unfailing, yields
   A calm sweet flow of placid peace and joy.

Below "Gibraltar" and the "Wigwam's" cone,
   And down below, where came the rudest shock,
The little rill kissed there a jutting stone,
   And smiling sweetly, called it "Mamie's Rock."

A zephyr whispered, " Pause, sweet stream, and tell
   Why thou hast o'er the field of battle flown,
Swept by ten thousand rocks, with gentle swell,
   And come down here to name this one alone.

"Is this one all that worthy is of name?
   A grand encampment, martial shaped, stands near,
And hosts of giants that might notice claim,
   Yet thou hast swept by all and lingered here."

The rill replied, in accents soft and sweet,
"They all were rough and rude, and as I came,
With frowns alone did they my coming greet;
A smile this gave, and I'll give it a name.

"Let rude, rough men, so like the rocks themselves,
Name all the others, I shall name but this;
No trysting-place be it for hideous elves,
Sweet name I give and baptize with a kiss.

"'Tis no rude, uncouth monster, frowning down
On me, as if my murmured song to hush,
Nor wears its dark, forbidding, threatening frown,
As if all near it it would gladly crush.

"'Tis not suggestive of 'grim-visaged war,'
Like wigwam or the stately tented field,
Nor stands it, like Gibraltar, as a bar,
Which to sweet influence disdains to yield.

"'Tis not like towering cliff nor gloomy cave,
The one to typify disgusting pride,
The other shelter giving every knave
Who chooses in its dismal depths to hide.

"'Tis not like these, but more like white-winged elf
That comes to soothe and cheer, and not to mock;
'Tis firm, but calm, a type of virtue's self,
And this is why I name it 'Mamie's Rock.'

"Misfortune 'tis (I will not say 'tis fate)
  That gems neglected lie in every land,
For soulless men can ne'er appreciate
  The treasures which they do not understand.

"I name this rock, and thus would I proclaim,
  O'er fancy's figments, sentiment and art,
That there is in a soft and lovely name
  A world of purity of soul and heart.

"Go, zephyr, find a maid whose name it bears,
  And tell her that it was ordained of yore
That fairies should the good protect from snares,
  And that the pure should ever love the pure.

"Tell her the murmuring rill has here and now,
  Without one fear of scowl or frown or blame,
Leaped up and kissed the lips, the cheeks, the brow,
  Of this fair rock and given it her name.

"And tell her, gentle zephyr, tell her, too,
  To be through life, at every time and place,
To her sweet self and all heart-promptings true,
  And firm as 'Mamie's Rock' upon its base."

The zephyr gave the promise,—then the rill,
  Which came relief to bring from tempest's shock,
Smiled calmly, sweetly, yet it lingered still,
  To guard and lave the base of "Mamie's Rock."

And there it lingers now though years have flown,
  And there amid surroundings all sublime,
Still claiming Mamie's Rock as all its own,
  'Twill linger fondly till the end of time.

THOU WILT REMEMBER.

THOUGH the sun be beaming brightly,
  Scattering scintillations 'round,
While the zephyrs float by lightly,
  And sweet flowers deck the ground,
All conspire to please and gladden,
And there's naught the heart to sadden,
Yet, a phantom form will rise,
And thy bright unwilling eyes
May with frowns be overcast
When to memory comes the past,—
All the pleasures we have known
In the days forever flown ;
For in May or cold December,
Thou canst never but remember,—
          Yes, remember !

When thy heart to me was given,—
  And that heart I thought was true,—
And I caught a glimpse of heaven
  When thy love for me I knew,

Ah! I rose to heights supernal,
Dreamed of happiness eternal,
Banished thoughts of pain and care,
For thy smile was on me there,
Beaming with the light of love,
Pure as that which lives above;
Then I held thy hand in mine,
And thou saidest, "I am thine!"
Ah! when comes each calm September,
Well I know thou wilt remember,—
          Yes, remember!

From thy heart I now am banished,
  And the hopes that once were mine,
All like molten snow have vanished
  (Lived and died by words of thine),—
Hopes that once thou bad'st me cherish,
But hast bidden now to perish;
Yet thy life will smoothly glide,
Thou wilt be another's bride,
And thy way will all be bright,
While I grope in gloom of night,
Mourning over love's last ember;
But I know thou wilt remember,—
          Yes, remember!

By and by when I am sleeping,
  And the vines above me wave,
Or the lonely willow, weeping,
  Marks my peaceful, welcome grave,

Now and then will rise before thee,
When the meditative mood comes o'er thee,
Many an unforgotten scene,
Which from view sod cannot screen;
Then thy still warm heart will know
All the harshness of the blow.
Be it April or September;
Sadly then thou wilt remember,—
        Yes, remember!

'TWAS ALL A DREAM.

'TWAS all a dream, I know it now; oh! would I might have had
This knowledge sooner, then the blow had been perhaps less sad;
Less painful, too, the waking from a dream, alas! too fleet;
Less bitter, and of what to me was so intensely sweet.

But thy sweet lips have spoken out, and my lone heart has heard
The sentence of my banishment, the cold and bitter word
Which cancels all, and me excludes from thy pure peerless heart,
And bids the hopes that once were sweet forever hence depart.

I utter no complaint, dear one; thou ne'er wilt hear from
  me,
What in my heart I cannot feel, one unkind word of
  thee;
I blame thee not, though deep the wound, and know I
  never will,
But, though I know 'tis hopeless, I must ever love thee
  still.

Oh! give me but one loving thought, nor cast me quite
  away;
To know that I am loved by thee would much of pain
  allay.
I ask thee not to bless my love, for this thou wilt not do,
Yet freely I have given thee devotion fond and true.

I may not look into thine eyes, which stoic's heart
  would move,
I may not hear again thy voice in soft sweet words of
  love;
And I may sorrow yet for years, that all the love that
  burned
Within my heart discarded is, although 'twas once re-
  turned.

But when I shall have passed away, and in earth's
  bosom sleep,
And few indeed above the mound where I shall slumber
  weep,
Oh! wilt thou not in mem'ry of the unforgotten year,
When thou and I so fondly loved, drop there one
  pearly tear?

Refuse me not this boon, dear one, nor let it prove a task
To grant to me this one request, 'tis all that I shall ask;
I would not cloud thy lovely brow nor sadden thy pure heart,
No, no, the sorrow all be mine, that hope and I must part.

If e'er at rosy eventide thou be'st in solitude,
And o'er thee softly, gently, steal a meditative mood,
Should in thy meditations come remembrance of my love,
Let not the sad reflection, then, thy heart to anger move.

I may, perhaps, be hov'ring o'er or watching by thy side,
And striving in my spirit-form thy footsteps here to guide;
For if the disembodied feel up there as they did here,
I know where'er thou art, dear one, my spirit will be near.

Then ere I go, oh! wilt thou not one sweet memento give?
To be to me a priceless prize to cherish while I live,
To be to me a soothing balm whene'er I come to die,
A recollection joyful in the coming by and by.

And that memento which I ask is but a word from thee,
A simple word of tenderness and love, dear one, for me;

Then thou wilt think less sadly of the deep, pure love
    I gave,
When I am calmly sleeping in my cold and narrow
    grave.

"THE DAYS THAT ARE NO MORE."

Dedicated as a mark of profound respect to a new-found lady
friend.

> " * * * * * * * *
> Tears from the depth of some divine despair
> Rise in the heart and gather in the eyes,
> In looking on the happy autumn fields,
> And thinking of the days that are no more."
>   TENNYSON.

AH, yes! unbidden tears will sadly rise,
To fill with misty haze the brightest eyes,
Tell of the pain that they have left behind,
Within the heart that fain relief would find,
When, glancing backward, memory lingers o'er,
In silent thought, " the days that are no more."

The friends of other years, from whom to part
Dull pain entailed and sorrow on the heart;
The dear ones whom we ne'er shall meet again,
The ties of love, now snapt, alas! in twain,—
These all come back, and seem, as heretofore
In happy days, " the days that are no more."

Sad memory many a lovely garland weaves,
Discards the withered flow'rs and russet leaves,
Adopts the fresh and bright, the cheerful green,
As typical of each delightful scene
The heart once knew, but time can ne'er restore,
For they were in "the days that are no more."

There is a sadness, yet a sweetness, too,
In memories that bring the past to view,
The unforgotten friends, the tender ties,
The soft, sweet words of love, the sparkling eyes,
The beaming smiles that friendly faces wore,
Now gone, with all "the days that are no more."

These mem'ries all are sadly sweet, and yet
I would that I the past might ev'n forget,
For oft it comes to me on darkened wings,
And some deep, bitter draught of poison brings,
Some wound received which vainly I deplore
When come to mind "the days that are no more."

All vain the wish! forgetfulness will not
The sombre scenes from mem'ry's tablet blot;
But, ah! the time is swiftly coming when
'Twill bring the coveted relief, and then
I, too, shall be—all earthly troubles o'er—
Forgotten with "the days that are no more."

A REFLECTION.

Some one has said (how truly said
　Let those who read reflect and say),
We'll clearer see when they are dead
　The worth of friends we love to-day.
We look now in their glowing eyes,
　And feel our kind impulses move;
We may, perchance, their friendship prize,
　And find a pleasure in their love;
But sometimes do we not refuse
　To speak the words they long to hear,
And, with a calm or cold excuse,
　Wound deeply those who hold us dear?

We may not think to give them pain,—
　The pain we give we may not see,—
But they will strive, alas! in vain,
　When mem'ries come, content to be;
For in their trusting hearts will live
　The fire of love, and death alone
Relief from mem'ry's pangs can give,—
　For in the grave no sorrow's known.
They uncomplaining bear, perchance,
　Nor breathe nor harbor thought of blame,
Receive the cold, unloving glance
　Which tells them, "Friendship's but a name."

And sometimes, when we silence break,
    And voice our thoughts, do not we then
Too carelessly or coldly speak
    The words that leave a rankling pain?
Oh! think awhile, that those who hear
    The calm, cold words in silent grief
Must patiently, though sadly, bear,
    Nor hope that time will bring relief.
Alas! the wounded ones will wait
    And bear, as only bear the brave;
Relief will come, but, ah! too late,—
    They only find it in the grave.

Why should we only prize when lost
    The friends whose love-fires brightly burn,
Who cherish us and love us most,
    And only ask a sweet return?
Why should we not all freely give
    The love which light and bliss will shed?
And why not give it while they live?
    'Twill yield no joy when they are dead.
Refuse not loving words to speak,
    For these can sweeten every sigh,
Where cold indiff'rence hearts will break,
    And leave the loving one to die.

WHATEVER IS IS BEST.

These verses are dedicated to her who requested me to write them.

"THE sun comes up and the sun goes down,"
    The busy world moves on apace,
We meet a smile and we meet a frown
    As here and there we see a face;
We meet the halt, the maimed, and the blind,
    See emblems both of peace and strife,
And, as we journey along, we find
    All phases here of human life;
They make us know and they make us see
    That some feel cursed, while few feel blest,
And yet 'twould different seem if we
    Could know whatever is is best.

We meet the rich and we meet the poor,
    For both are all around us here;
We see the prince and we see the boor,
    And each is lordly in his sphere;
We see the wicked, we see the good,
    The rains alike on both descend;
One raises strife and the other food,
    And thus 'twill be till time shall end;

And as we grope or hurry along,
  We pause anon to think and rest,
And wonder oft if the busy throng
  Believe whatever is is best.

We meet with friends and we meet with foes,
  For this is but the lot of all,
And fortune comes and fortune goes,
  As what goes up we know must fall;
And when with smiles or with frowns we meet,
  Let's one enjoy, the other bear,
For life with either were incomplete
  Unless the other, too, was there;
There's certainly use for all and room,—
  Ev'n reptiles rosy bow'rs infest,—
And oh! 'twould banish much of life's gloom
  To feel whatever is is best.

I sit alone and I sigh alone,
  The sky above wears now a frown,
The night is dark, and the daylight gone,
  And the rain is pattering down;
And yet I know from far o'er that sky,
  Ev'n though not a star I can see,
The same one sleepless, all-seeing eye
  Keeps watch o'er my loved ones and me.
I pine for dear ones far, far away,
  Yet sweet I know will be the rest
In which, in my dreams, I'll hear them say,
  "Believe whatever is is best."

"JESUS WEPT."

Oh, wondrous love! Earth never knew
    The like of this before,—
A love so pure, divine, and true,—
    And ne'er can know it more;
And well might angels' anthems blend
When "Jesus wept" above his friend.

Oh, matchless love! The heaving breast,
    Wherein ne'er guile had dwelt,
Poured forth the stream of deep unrest,
    The anguish that it felt,
When o'er the grave where Laz'rus slept
The great Redeemer bowed and wept.

Oh, priceless love! The sun might well
    Withdraw his shining head
When sacred tears like dew-drops fell
    Above the slumb'ring dead;
No wonder that the dead should rise
When tear-drops flowed from Jesus' eyes.

Oh, love divine! Let heaven ring
    With loud and long acclaim,
And all earth's countless thousands sing
    Hosannas to His name,—
Hosanna to the God above,
Whose nature and whose name is love.

Oh, deathless love! Be't thine and mine
  This priceless boon to share,
To kneel before the throne divine
  And worship sweetly there,
And know for aye all doubts and fears
Are washed away by Jesus' tears.

FOUND! LOST!

THERE'S many a gem that hidden lies
  Behind some stone, or wall, or screen,
Beyond the reach of human eyes,
  Until, by accident, 'tis seen.

By accident? Nay, Heaven's laws
  Man's fortunes sway by more than this;
Effect is always due to cause,
  And so with human woe or bliss.

But when the gem—however found—
  First sparkles on his ravished view,
He feels, though Fortune long has frowned,
  She may again her smiles renew.

He dreams a dream of sweet delight,
  And fancies naught can come to mar
The vision, which appears as bright
  As Heaven's beauteous evening star.

Perchance his dream may end in bliss,
　　Perchance alone in bitter woe;
Deep disappointment—only this—
　　It *may* be his, alas! to know.

He yields his heart and all his soul
　　To one who smiles when he is near;
Submissive bows to her control,
　　And trusts—with ne'er a doubt or fear.

But, ah! when he is far away,
　　Weighed down, perhaps, by toil and care,
Though in his bosom, night and day,
　　His loved one holds dominion there,

Then she, the worshipped one, perhaps
　　Surrounded by admiring throngs,
Has even let her memory lapse
　　While listening to their sweeter songs.

He feels, though he has found a gem
　　So pure and so serenely bright,
That only Heaven's diadem
　　Can parallel its beauteous light.

He soon, alas! must lose again
　　That which was more than life to him,
For she, with silent, cold disdain,
　　Has filled his chalice to the brim;

That chalice, too, which at her touch ·
Had with the nect'rine juices flown,
Delighting heart and soul, and such
As he before had never known.

Oh, is his precious jewel lost!
His heart a prey to sorrow's sighs?
His brightest, sweetest dream a ghost?
Then, angel one, he calmly dies.

LITTLE HETTY.

GENTLE Hetty, winsome lassie,
    Would I might a garland weave—
Weave for thee—of fragrant flowers,
    Culled at early spring-time eve.

'Round thy brow I would entwine it,
    Bright in all its varied hues,
Sweet in fragrance, soft in beauty,
    Fresh in evening's pearly dews.

And I'd have it emblematic,
    Thy pure life to typify;
Sweeter, brighter growing ever,
    Perfect in the by and by.

Not a blossom in it fading,
  Not a leaf should from it fall;
Highest virtues representing,
  Thou shouldst beautify them all.

Beautify by sweetly showing
  How the virtues all may shine,
'Mid corruption life surrounding,
  And that all, sweet one, are thine.

Gentle Hetty, Heaven bless thee,
  Keep all tear-drops from thine eyes,
Guard and guide through life, and give thee
  Then a home beyond the skies.

Years from now when I am sleeping,
  If thy glance should linger here,
Give to friendship and affection
  Mem'ry's tribute then,—a tear.

WOMEN'S VOWS.

Some women's vows are like the reeds
  That bend beneath the blast,
Still lower, as the tempest speeds,
  And snap in twain at last;

And he who shall on them rely,
  When most support he needs,
Will find, with sorrow, by and by,
  They are but broken reeds.

Some women's vows like footprints are
  Upon the sandy shore,
Which, when the billows revel there,
  Are seen again no more;
And he who on those tracks depends
  For guidance o'er the strand,
Will, ere his wand'ring journey ends,
  Be far from hope and land.

And some are like the flecks of spray
  That on the waters lie,
Which, when the tempest sweeps that way,
  Before the blasts will fly;
And he who with this foam shall think
  To cool his burning mouth,
Will find, whene'er he stoops to drink,
  It nothing is but froth.

But some, thank God! are like the lights
  That glimmer in the sky,
Which still beam on through darkest nights,
  Though hidden from the eye;
And he who shall confiding look,
  And wait and watch afar,
When by the world and all forsook,
  Will see his guiding star.

These are not like the brittle reed,
  But like the solid rocks,
Which neither cloud nor tempest heed,
  But stand their rudest shocks;
And he who on such rocks finds rest
  Shall never feel alarm,
For he will be supremely blest,
  And free from every harm.

THE DIGNITY OF LABOR.

To crave and worship what is fine
  Has come to be a passion,—
To bow and kneel before the shrine
  Of wealth and show and fashion,—
And men and women, all, applaud
  The ways of wealth and folly,
And palliate the darkest fraud
  With soothing melancholy;
Excuse is made for wrong and stealth
  (His virtues overrated),
Whene'er by one of solid wealth
  The act is perpetrated;
They say 'twas but a "freak," a "whim,"
  Of nature frank and mellow;
"There's surely nothing wrong in him:
  He is too good a fellow."

But let the guilty man be poor,—
  Though ever so deserving,
And though the wolf was at his door,
  And wife and babes were starving,—
The world will no excuses brook;
  It taunts him in his anguish,
And leaves him, for the loaf he took,
  In prison walls to languish;
No gentle accents reach his ear,
  No eye-glance shows compassion,
Naught comes the dungeon's gloom to cheer,
  For " it is not the fashion ;"
And yet—whate'er the world may say,
  Though cutting be its coldness,
And gold and fashion rule the day,
  And vaunt their sway with boldness—
There's many a modest artisan,
  And many a working-woman,
And many a worthy lab'ring man,
  The peer of " noblest Roman ;"
And these, though wealth they may not know,
  Will stand by friend or neighbor,
And by unblemished lives will show
  The dignity of labor.

A *true man* will not duty shirk,
  But he will learn to love it,
Nor will he be ashamed of work,
  Nor hold himself above it;

Though fools may (for his want of pelf)
    Treat coldly and reject him,
Yet, if he but respect himself,
    True men will all respect him;
"The rank is but the guinea's stamp;"
    If man is true "and a' that,"—
A workingman, no idle tramp,—
    He'll honor win "and a' that;"
He need not dread the idler's scorn,
    For there is nothing in it;
To fame no man was ever born,—
    He who would wear must win it.

Stand up! ye men who live by work,
    Who nobly earn your wages;
Ye women, who no duty shirk,
    Your ranks have nurtured sages;
The glitt'ring gold will come and go,
    And friends it oft estranges,
And fashion is but tinsel show,
    Which every season changes;
Your own good hands will bring you bread,
    And all you need substantial,
Nor have you fashion's whims to dread,
    Nor hurricanes financial;
The world may frown a little while,
    But this is surely better
Than see its sycophantic smile,
    And have it fawn and flatter.
But 'twill not always on you frown,
    If you assert,—and prove it,—

Misfortune cannot put you down,
    And proudly rise above it ;
That gold, with all its fawning clan
    And sycophants attendant,
Can ne'er o'er-ride an honest man,
    Upright and independent.

Do not your friendly aid deny
    To fellow-men and brothers,
Nor cast a wistful, envious eye
    On what belongs to others ;
Enjoy the good, by fortune sent,
    Nor covet show nor treasure,
For peace of mind and sweet content
    Yield more substantial pleasure.
If you, perchance, injustice meet
    From fellow-man or woman,
Forgiveness is divine and sweet,
    While error is but human ;
Remember this, and never be
    To erring friends uncivil ;
Forgive, forget, and let them see
    You good return for evil ;
Teach them the principles of love,
    The virtues of religion,
Forgiveness, as they're taught above,
    In heaven's sinless region,
Where all is peaceful, bright, and fair,
    Fraternal, kind, and loving,
And countless hosts of ransomed are
    Through fields Elysian roving ;

Thus shall you win from error's ways,
    When friendship else had perished,
Those who, through many happy days,
    You lovingly have cherished.

Be to yourselves and honor true;
    Be firm, yet not defiant;
And, when the world shall see that you
    Are proudly self-reliant,
The horny hand, the punctured tips,
    The sun-browned face and sooty,
The modest garb, the frost-chapped lips,
    The lab'rer true to duty,
Will never then a coldness know
    From stranger or from neighbor,
For all will pay due honor to
    The dignity of labor.

ONE BY ONE.

One by one around us sleeping,
    Lie the friends of other years,—
Friends o'er whom were vain the weeping,
    Sorrow's silent, briny tears;
Yes, ah, yes! the weeping o'er them,
    Now, alas! is only vain,
For our tears can ne'er restore them
    Back to us on earth again.

But until we, too, shall perish,
    And, like them, in death shall sleep,
We those loved ones still may cherish,
    And 'mong mem'ry's jewels keep;
Keep them there, and though regretting—
    Sorr'wing—that 'twas Heaven's will
They should go, yet ne'er forgetting
    We can love them fondly still.

Nor, were we endowed with power,
    Would we bid those loved ones come
Back from that celestial bower,
    Where is now their peaceful home.
Here they sleep, but there immortal,—
    Deathless as the God who reigns,—
They have entered heaven's portal,
    And are chanting rapt'rous strains.

And while we their mem'ries treasure,
    And their deeds of love recall,
Find a melancholy pleasure
    In recounting each and all.
More than this we have in feeling,
    As we thus review the past,—
Faith a deathless hope revealing,—
    That we'll meet again at last.

Thus, when comes calm retrospection,
    And I think of friends at rest,
Sweet to me is this reflection,—
    They are now supremely blest;

Blest in freedom from all sorrow,
    From all sickness, pain, and care,
Blest to-day and blest to-morrow
    And for evermore up there.

SHADOW AND SUNSHINE.

'TIS sweet to think that care and pain,
    And all the memories that fling
Dark shadows o'er the heart's domain,
    Will some time, soon or late, take wing;
That all the clouds that dim life's sky,
    The canopy to mar and blot,
Will, in the coming by and by,
    Pass from that sky and be forgot.

And ev'n the fickle stars, that glide
    'Twixt heaven's summit and its rim,
And now and then their twinklings hide,
    Will, in the course of time, grow dim;
Yet there are stars, all fixed and bright,
    Which, in the vaulted sky, for aye
Will beam amid the gloom of night,
    Till sky and time shall pass away.

Then let the heart be bravely nerved
    The stings of cruelty to bear,
The bitter wrongs all undeserved,
    Which proofs of fickle natures are,—

For conscience can the load uplift,
   Can smile and hum a cheerful song,
Can banish sneers and frowns adrift;
   It knows it guiltless is of wrong.

Some friends—nay, nay, can those be friends
   Who smile upon us when we may
Be useful to them, but, when ends
   Our usefulness, will turn away?—
Will wound the hearts that held them dear,
   And in their truthfulness believed,
That friendly words were wont to hear,
   Nor dreamed that they could be deceived.

Yet, there are friends who never change,
   Whose hearts are like the sun on high,
Which naught can from the right estrange
   Or banish from the azure sky;
And these the peerless jewels are
   Of all earth's purest gems that shine,
They rival heaven's brightest star,
   And some such friends, thank God, are mine.

Then bear up, wronged and wounded heart,
   Nor let cold, fickle fortune's frown
Again the scar with bleeding start,
   Nor like a burden press thee down;
Be true, as thou hast ever been,
   To those who truest are to thee,
And though deep sorrows thou hast seen,
   Thy future will all brighter be.

THE BEAUTIFUL SOUTH.

The South! fair and lovely and beautiful South!
   I do not sing now of the land of my birth,
But a nymph with brown eyes and beautiful mouth,—
   A flower as lovely as grows upon earth.
Her smile's like a sun-ray that flits o'er the skies,
   Her voice like the music of angelic choirs,
And bright as the stars are her beautiful eyes,
   Yet brighter they'll be when illumed by love's fires.

The South! ever-blooming and beautiful South!
   I sing not the land where magnolias throw
Perfume on the air through the long summer's drouth,
   And lilies and roses and jessamines grow;
No, no; these are sweet, and their beauties they bring
   To decorate Southland spring, summer, and fall,
Yet 'tis not of this nor of these that I sing:
   A South is my theme sweeter far than them all.

The South! gem of loveliness, beautiful South!
   That hearts hence will wound or will cause to rejoice,
By glance of her eye or by words of her mouth,
   Her frown or her smile or the tone of her voice;
Ah! this the South that my muse has in view,
   The South in whose honor a song she would sing,
The South she believes to be artless and true,
   The South unto whom she a tribute would bring.

The South! incomp'rable fair South, at whose shrine
  The hearts of the gallant, the brave, and the true
Do homage, and garlands around it entwine
  Of myrtle and roses and hyacinths blue;
May ever the beauty that tints her fair brow,
  The soft, glowing light that illumines her eye,
Her heart, and her life be as peerless as now,
  And perfect her bliss in "the sweet by and by."

THE FARMER'S CORN AND MINE.

The farmer's smiles are broad and bright
  When he, in early morn
(Provided seasons have been right),
  Looks on his growing corn;
And when 'tis growing rich and fine
  His heart o'erflows with glee,—
His corn gives him delight, but mine
  Provokes no smile from me.

When summer ploughing all is done
  The farmer, feeling blest,
Gives all his "hands" a day of fun,
  His "teams" a day of rest;
His bosom never heaves a sigh,
  We never hear him moan,
He's jolly o'er his corn, while I,
  O'er mine, fret, writhe, and groan.

When winter comes the farmer's corn
  Is safely stored away,
And he's contented night and morn
  And through the wintry day;
He has enough for food, he knows,
  And happy is his lot,
While, though I've corn which onward grows,
  Yet happy I am not.

I envy not, yet I would be,
  Through all the days and years,
As happy and content as he,
  But my corn causes tears;
The cause of difference in the yield
  Of pleasure and of woe,—
His corn is in his barn and field,
  While mine is on my toe.

A VISION.

I saw her once,—too briefly then,
  And still, in fancy, see her now,—
All radiant in her beauty, when
  No cloud nor shade obscured her brow;
Across that brow serenely played
  A bright and sportive sunny beam;
I wondered could the vision fade,
  As often fades a poet's dream.

Her soft brown eyes were calmly bright,
   Her face, as face of houri, fair,
And o'er it shone celestial light,
   For happy smiles were playing there;
And that fair brow, which, ne'er before,
   Had met my eager, curious gaze,
Was something angels might adore,
   And scan its beauty in amaze.

I wondered then, I wonder now,
   And so shall wonder many a day,
Why 'tis so beautiful a brow
   From sight is ever hid away.
No vision e'er appeared to me
   Like this, my weary eyes to bless;
Nor had I ever hoped to see
   So fair a gem of loveliness.

Yet, there she stood, a very queen,
   Her eyes with soft, sweet light ablaze,
Her face as autumn sky serene,
   While I could only stand and gaze.
But ah! 'tis one of nature's laws
   That ev'n the worm, which dies so soon,
While grov'ling in the dust, may pause,
   And render homage to the moon.

That worm, although it now, perchance,
   May lift its fascinated eyes,
In one intense and ling'ring glance,
   Up to the queen of yonder skies,

To-morrow may have ceased to live;
   Or, living, it may writhe in pain,
And yet, it all of life would give
   To worship that pure moon again.

Perhaps the vision I have seen
   Again may never bless mine eyes,
Until I pass from things terrene
   To purer ones above the skies;
But in that world of fadeless light,
   The fairest 'mong the angels fair,
All sweetly robed in spotless white,
   I know that I shall see her there.

I KNOW NOT WHY.

I KNOW not why the storm-clouds cast
   Their dark and threat'ning shadows down,
Foretelling each a tempest blast
   Or flood that shall the herbage drown;
'Tis so, I've seen them oft and o'er,
   Seen lightnings flash across the sky,
Heard Heaven's grand artill'ry roar;
   I know they come, but know not why.

I know not why the sun at day,
   The calm, sweet silver moon at night,
Comes each in turn to fling its ray
   O'er earth, imparting life and light;

And yet 'tis so, I've seen these too,
　The one when turquoise curtain high
O'erhangs, the other when the blue
　Is hidden; yet, I know not why.

I know not why the flowers bloom,
　Or why the birds so sweetly sing,
Or whence their pow'r to lighten gloom,
　And cheerfulness o'er earth to fling;
And yet, I've seen the blooming flow'rs,
　Heard sweet bird-music floating by,
Have felt their soft mysterious pow'rs
　Upon me, but I know not why.

I know not why the fleeting breath—
　Which like the softest zephyr flies—
Alone, the strong man shields from death,
　And when it ceases, then he dies;
But I have seen ev'n this, alas!
　Have seen my loved ones calmly die,
Have watched the final moment pass,
　And know 'tis so, but know not why.

Yet this the secret is of all:
　There is a mighty ruling hand,
An eye that sees the sparrow fall,
　A pow'r that can the world command;
A King who reigns by night, by day,
　Who rules the earth, the sea, the sky,
Whom dead and living all obey
　When He commands, and this is why.

His voice is heard in thunders loud,
    In softest zephyrs floating by;
He rules the tempest and the cloud,
    And all the planets in the sky;
He speaks, and hosts unnumbered stand,
    His mighty arm supports them all;
He moves His strong protecting hand,
    And thousands upon thousands fall.

While this I feel, and this I know,
    I see around me day by day
A heedless class, who reckless go
    Along a broad and crooked way.
They know it leads to death—and where!
    And yet they wildly, onward fly
To ruin and to dark despair,
    Alas! alas! I know not why.

THE UNDECORATED GRAVES.

Ah! many a fallen hero sleeps
    Among the valleys, hills, and plains,
O'er whom no eye fond vigil keeps,
    Though mem'ry's casket still retains
Each well-loved name, and o'er it weeps,
    And will while love or life remains.

When spring-time, with its fragrance, comes,
    And smiling wood and field are clad
In brightest buds and sweetest blooms,
    And nature joyous seems and glad,
Naught then should darken loving homes;
    Yet lingers still one mem'ry sad.

We seek the spot where loved ones sleep,—
    Our cherished, unforgotten dead,
Whose mem'ries still we fondly keep,—
    And o'er them sweetest blossoms spread,
Which tell of love, sincere and deep,
    For each one in his lowly bed.

And then we turn, with deep-drawn sigh,
    With mind oppressed and saddened heart,
With laden breath and drooping eye,
    From which the heavy tear-drops start,
And think of other friends, who lie
    In graves unknown and far apart.

We think of those, and think with pain,—
    Which time has given calmer tone,—
That, though they fell on hill and plain
    Where they their heroism had shown,—
Fell bravely, 'mong the hapless slain,—
    Their graves, alas! are all unknown.

In summer morning's misty light,
    While dew the tender herbage laves,

Or through the spring day, softly bright,
    While corn its silken tassel waves,
The cattle, in their dumb delight,
    Browse o'er those long-neglected graves.

And yet the sleepers all were true;
    No truer, braver men than they;
Brave those who wore the Union blue
    And those who wore the Southern gray;
Though we may know not—never knew—
    Where they are sleeping, far away.

My loving muse would, for those braves
    (For all, and not my friends alone),—
Glad that one banner only waves
    And fratricidal war is done,—
A tribute spread upon the graves
    Undecorated and unknown.

TO RUTH.

On the reception of a beautiful souvenir wrought for me by her own fair hands.

My fair, sweet, gentle friend, I knew
    That 'mong the many birds that sang,
The countless lovely flow'rs that grew,
    And all the charming girls that bang,

There was not bird, nor flow'r, nor girl
  More fair and beautiful than thou,
Yet did not know thou wert the pearl—
  The gem—that I have found thee now.

Thy beauty I could plainly see,—
  And thee I do not flatter, Ruth,—
But beauty rarely seems to be
  The soul of purity and truth;
Anon 'tis but a flimsy veil
  That hides defects behind a smile,
And then 'tis like a coat of mail
  That grievous faults obscure awhile.

Some striking beauties I have known,
  And now and then I one have seen
Who seemed to be a paragon
  Of womankind, a very queen;
I seemed in such an one to see
  Pure gold refined—without alloy,—
But, ah! I erred, yet only she
  The inspiration could destroy.

While beauty, both of form and face,
  A radiant brow and sparkling eyes,
A gentle manner, easy grace,
  May constitute, indeed, a prize,
Yet these but for a while awake
  A fancy that too brief may be;
They ne'er a peerless woman make,
  Whose soul is not sincerity.

And thus thou seest, gentle Ruth,
  That beauty does not always blend
With changeless constancy and truth,—
  At least, I so have found, fair friend,—
Yet thou hast clearly shown to me
  A character almost divine,
That truth and beauty blend in thee,
  And both are eminently thine.

Thy gift, my gentle friend, I take,
  And I shall keep and prize it long,
And for its beauty and thy sake
  Would it embalm in deathless song;
But nothing my poor muse can bring
  Could with thy beauteous gift compare,
And yet 'tis from my heart I sing,
  And thou and it I'll cherish there.

May softest sunlight o'er thee shine
  Along life's pathway to its end,
And disappointments that are mine
  Be never known to thee, sweet friend.
May friends be always what they seem,
  And nothing e'er their hearts estrange,
But may they all, till ends life's dream,
  Be true to thee, and free from change.

Be happy, thou, through all thy days,
  No sorrow come nor gloom nor strife,
No frowning brow e'er meet thy gaze
  To mar the sweetness of thy life.

God bless thee, Ruth; I'll think of thee,
And give thee fond affection, too;
Forget me not, and ever be
To thy sweet self and virtue true.

"SOME TIME."

Dedicated to a fair lady who said she intended to sit for her picture, and would give me a copy. When? "Some time."

THE flowers faded long ago;
They sweetly bloomed awhile, and then
They drooped and withered, but I know
That "some time" they will bloom again,—
Yes, "some time" they will catch the dews,
And on the air their fragrance fling,
Stand forth arrayed in beauty's hues
To decorate the brow of Spring.

The visions we have seen in dreams,
That made us smile or made us weep,
Wore cloudy scowls or sunny beams,
To discompose or sweeten sleep,
Will "some time" come again to view,
And, as before, perhaps, will wear
A rosy or a sombre hue,
Foretelling pleasure or despair.

The clouds that hide the sun to-day,
  And o'er the earth their shadows cast,
Will soon or "some time" pass away,
  For gloom and shadows cannot last;
And when the clouds have floated by,
  The sun will come with radiant glow
To gild the overarching sky
  And gladden all the world below.

These all will be, and "some time," too,
  I'll own a bright artistic gem,—
A copy of a fair friend, who
  Would grace a throne and diadem;
And she in person, not in art,
  Will "some time," with angelic mien,
Hold empire in some manly heart
  And reign its undisputed queen.

Could I but haste time's rolling car,
  For once I'd cause its wheels to move
With all the speed of shooting-star
  That darts across the skies above;
I'd give the fleeting moments wing,
  To swifter fly than e'er they flew,
That they to me should sooner bring
  The "some time" and that picture, too.

GONE TO THAT FAIR LAND.

A tribute to the memory of Miss Hattie B. Frick, late of Evansville, Indiana. The last two times she sang in public her songs were "Dost Thou Know that Fair Land?" "Let Me Go; Let Me Go."—*Commercial Gazette.*

THE tuneful voice, which erst the thousands thrilled,
   And wakened echoes in each heart, is now
In death's deep, gloomy silence calmly stilled,
   And snowy cold that erewhile beauteous brow,—
Nay, beauteous still, for though death's mark is there,
   Its pow'r to wreck such beauty could but fail,
And o'er a brow so lovely and so fair
   It could not fling a dark, obscuring veil.

That voice, attuned, while here, to sweetest song,
   Is filled up yonder with celestial fire,
To rise and float in rapt'rous strains among,
   And be the sweetest in, the sacred choir;
Too rich and pure it was for earth alone,
   Too sweet for mortal ears alone to hear,
Its echoes reached the great eternal throne,
   And now resound within that holier sphere.

The sweetest flow'r that blooms in early spring,
   And sips the dews that fall from balmy skies,
Its fragrant odors all abroad to fling,
   In burning, dewless heat of summer dies;

But then we know, whene'er to see it droop
  O'erwhelms our sympathetic hearts with pain,
That, one among a bright and lovely group,
  We yet shall see it sweetly bloom again.

The morning star, which, in expiring night,
  The wand'rer through the dismal forest cheers,
And which at darkest hour is grandly bright,
  In heaven's beauty melts when dawn appears;
That orb which never yet has been untrue,
  And in night's deepest gloom ne'er fails to come,
Although it now be hid awhile from view,
  Is shining still within its far-off home.

We know the stars that shine to cheer night's gloom,
  To live and shine forever, were not made,
And all the sweetest, fairest flowers that bloom
  Are destined in a little while to fade;
These all will pass away, and yet the soul
  Outlives, by countless ages, fleeting breath,
And seeks and finds its high, immortal goal
  Alone, beyond the narrow stream of death.

And this bright star, that 'lumined earth awhile,
  This lovely flow'r that bloomed to give delight,
This bird of song, now basks in heaven's smile,
  Where neither winter comes nor gloomy night;
And as the anthems swell in sweetest song
  The echoes of the past come soft and low,
The loved one sings, amid the seraph throng,
  In "That Fair Land" to which she longed to go.

BROWN EYES.

AH! brown eyes, beauteous brown eyes, when kind
    nature, rich and free,
Gave lovely brow and rosy lips and bright brown eyes
    to thee,
A form of perfect mould and grace and tender, loving
    heart,
She gave her gifts right royally, and smiled at works
    of art;
She knew her gifts, indeed, would all those tinsel things
    outvie,
That they would captivate the heart, and more than
    please the eye,
That they would be the living stamp of beauty and of
    worth,
And make of thee a priceless pearl, an angel here on
    earth.

And, brown eyes, gentle brown eyes, the beauties that
    are thine,
The bird-like voice, the rippling laugh, the form so
    near divine,
The soft, sweet smile, the thrilling glance, the bright,
    bewitching face,
The winsome ways, the bright brown eyes, and every
    perfect grace,

The art of giving pleasure, and the happy, joyous
  mood,
Were given, gentle brown eyes, all for purposes of
  good,
Were given, not alone for thy heart's own happiness,
But were given, freely given, other loving ones to bless.

I've sometimes thought a smiling bud the sweetest ever
  made,
And sighed to think that every flow'r that blooms, alas!
  must fade;
I've gazed upon the blazing sun, and seen his light
  grow dim
As down the western sky he stepped, behind its rosy rim;
I've watched the moon upon her throne in placid calm-
  ness proud,
And I have seen her beauties hid behind a floating
  cloud;
I've seen the sky aglow with stars, bright, beautiful,
  and clear,
And I have seen those twinkling gems at day-dawn
  disappear.

But when the flower's leaves have all around me with-
  ered lain,
I've known that 'neath the summer sun 'twould bud
  and bloom again;
And when I've seen the sun at eve in splendor pass
  away,
I knew to-morrow he would shine as brightly as to-
  day;

The moon so calm, so brightly sweet, though hidden for awhile,
I knew would soon again appear upon the world to smile,
And every star that through night's gloom the sky made bright and fair,
Though hid in daylight, when night came would shine as sweetly there.

So, brown eyes, with thy beauty; it is something that will live,
A pure delight and happiness to loving hearts to give;
A gem, though hid, perchance, awhile will glitter yet again,
Imparting pleasure or, perhaps, alleviating pain;
A flow'r that, though its leaves should fade and wither at my feet,
I know would ere long bloom again as beautifully sweet,
For I within those brown eyes read a purity of soul
Which, in the fleeting present, ne'er can reach its destined goal.

Ah! brown eyes, gentle brown eyes, may soft love-light on thee beam,
Make bright thine every wakeful hour and sweet thine every dream;
May dimless sun-rays from thy sky drive every shade of gloom,
And beautiful and fragrant flow'rs along thy pathway bloom;

May some kind star thy footsteps guide away from
    toil and strife,
And peace and sweet contentment ever beautify thy
    life;
And, brown eyes, gentle brown eyes, my last fond wish
    is this,—
That here those eyes shall close at last to ope in realms
    of bliss.

WILL SHE, TOO, CHANGE?

(M——.)

I HAVE a friend, a fair young friend,—
  But friends I've thought I had before,
And trusted them until the end,
  And they, alas! were friends no more;
The changes came, I knew not how,
  I only know I thought it strange
That they should come at all,—but now,
  I wonder if this one will change?

She is a fair and gentle one,
  And truth is in her heart I know,
And even though she loves her fun,
  That heart can "feel another's woe;"
For though I ne'er have heard her sighs,
  Nor seen her deep distress endure,
I've gazed into her soft bright eyes,
  And know her heart is warm and pure.

And yet, and yet, the fickle flame,
  Which burns awhile and then goes out,—
And is alone an empty name,—
  Throws over all a cloud of doubt,
A fear that what seems now so bright,
  So pleasing to the heart and eye,
Will be, in more than gloom of night,
  Obscured forever, by and by.

But I would fain this friend believe,
  I would not—no, I will not—think
That one so gentle could deceive,
  Or coldly sever friendship's link;
Yet when, through all the misty past,
  The active, sleepless memories range,
The mental query comes at last:
  Will this one, too, like others, change?

I've learned to doubt, but not from choice;
  No, this my heart would never do,
But happily would it rejoice
  To feel that every friend is true;
That they from me, come weal or woe,
  No circumstance will e'er estrange,
And it is longing now to know
  If this fair, gentle friend will change.

The future I may not divine,
  The stars are mysteries to me,
I read no omen there, nor sign,
  Of what the future is to be;

But as my eyes on them to-night,
   Along the vaulted heavens range,
Faith seems inspir'd by their soft light,
   That this fair friend will never change.

"MOUSEY."

You think, perhaps, my Muse has come
   To sing a dainty song to-night,
To yonder little mouse whose home
   Is suited to the tiny mite.
If so you think, then you are wrong;
   I have a more inspiring theme,
One worthy of the sweetest song,
   And of the poet's brightest dream.

Her eyes are bright as glinting rays
   That shoot from cloudless summer sky,
When nature's laws the sun obeys,
   And moves in kingly state on high;
Her smile is like the blooming flow'r
   When sprinkled o'er with sparkling dew;
Her voice is soft, yet sweet in pow'r
   To stony, stubborn hearts subdue.

Her beauteous brow (as I suppose,
   For really that is seldom seen)
Bespeaks a mind in sweet repose,
   A conscience placid and serene;

A soul as pure as falling snow,
   And free from all disturbing pangs,—
I'm guessing this I own, for oh!
   That brow is hid behind her bangs.

Her heart—but then I am not sure
   She has a heart to call her own;
Yet, if so, it is warm and pure
   As e'er humanity has known;
And if she has this treasure lost,
   The finder will, if he be wise,
Be careful of it, and may boast
   That he has found a priceless prize.

A paragon in form and face,
   As beautiful in mind and heart,
She walks the earth with queenly grace,
   And nothing knows of guile or art.
Now, who is she? You'd like to know,
   And whether she is yet "engaged"?
I may not tell you either, though
   She is not like my mousey, caged.

Now look around, ye gallant boys:
   There's more in life than you may think;
Its cup contains substantial joys,
   Which you, if wise, may sometimes drink;
And happy, in supreme degree,
   And prouder than a sceptr'd king,
The one, among you all, will be
   Who traps the mousey whom I sing.

LENA LEE.

Though the night shades hang o'er me obscuring the skies,
Yet I see beaming on me a pair of bright eyes,
For darling, sweet daughter, I'm thinking of thee,
And feel thou art near me, my sweet Lena Lee.

The soft trilling tones of thy voice seem to fall
On my ear like sweet music, other days to recall,
And thy smile like a sunbeam the darkness dispels,
For where thou art, darling, only happiness dwells.

How I long to my bosom thy dear form to clasp,
And thy tiny soft hand in my rough one to grasp,
Fond affection's soft kiss on thy pure lips to press,
And receive on my own a far sweeter caress!

Oh! 'tis sweet to remember, though we are apart,
I retain an asylum in thy peerless heart,
And though others may frown or look coldly on me,
I am blessed in the love of my sweet Lena Lee.

Ah! my darling, could I but annihilate space,
Not a moment should pass ere we stood face to face,
Not a moment ere 'round thee my arms should entwine,
Not a moment ere thou wouldst embrace me in thine.

And I think of thee often, as I'm thinking now,
In my fancy gaze lovingly upon thy fair brow,
Hear the trill of thy laughter, thy musical voice,
And the vision buoys up my lone heart to rejoice.

Dost thou think of me, darling,—papa, far away,—
In the morn by the hearthstone, and eve at croquet?
And oh, little angel! when thou kneelest in prayer,
Is my form ever present, dear one, with thee there?

Never close I my eyelids in slumber at night,
Never go I abroad in the soft morning light,
Until, first, I have asked for a blessing on thee,
And the loving ones near thee, my sweet Lena Lee.

Heaven smile on thee, darling, and freely bestow
Every blessing upon thee, and shield thee from woe,
Smooth thy pathway through life, and at last bid thee rise
To a home everlasting above the blue skies.

Good-night now, my dear one, may thy slumbers be blest
With the visions alone that can sweeten thy rest;
May the angels of heaven keep ward over thee,
Through the night-time and always, my sweet Lena Lee.

MY BIRDIE HAS FLOWN.

The clouds this morn hang murky, dark, and low,
    And as I sit in silence all alone,
I look in vain for one sweet face, and know
    My birdie has away down southward flown.

Far, far away from others dear to me,
    She came, my irksome solitude to cheer,
And then, around, I fancied I could see
    The loved ones all, whenever she was near.

She gladdened these surrounding scenes awhile,
    And with her sweet companion made life bright,
For in her voice, and happy, sunny smile,
    Were cordials, giving comfort and delight.

As now and then across a clouded sky
    Stream glowing rays that banish gloom away,
So her sweet smile could soften every sigh,
    And gloom of night invest with light of day.

The church-bells sound their notes upon the air,
    And from their homes to solemn worship call
The thoughtful people, and to earnest prayer
    For gracious blessings and for good to all.

And they are cheerful, but, alas! to me
  The summons fails to cheerfulness restore;
It brings alone to saddened memory
  "The days," the bright, sweet days, "that are no more."

And now, whate'er I touch, whate'er I see,
  That she has ever touched or seen or known,—
Though dearer it has thus been made to me,—
  Reminds me that my gentle bird has flown.

May angels hover o'er and guard her still,
  As, lovingly, they in the past have done,
Her cup with sweets, and with these only, fill,
  Till those that flow eternally are won.

Sweet birdie mine, my loving heart would send,
  Through all the clouds and mists around above,
To thee, and all the dear ones, and thy friend,
  Its purest, warmest, undiluted love.

Remember me at every time and place,
  And when each heart goes out in earnest prayer,
Oh! bear my name before the throne of grace,
  And daily ask for me a blessing there.

'TIS BUT A FADED FLOWER.

'Tis but a faded flow'r you see,
  Its tints and fragrance all departed;
'Twas given in its bloom to me,
  By one as fair and happy-hearted;
But now, it withered, drooping hangs,
  Alone what once it was revealing,
As on her fair young brow the bangs
  Are beauties rich and rare concealing.

'Tis but a faded flow'r, and yet
  It calls to mind the pleasant greetings,
The kindly, friendly smiles I met
  Upon our first and second meetings;
The flow'r was beautiful and pure,
  Yet not more so than she who gave it,
And though 'tis faded, I am sure
  The dews of friendship long will lave it.

And years from now it will recall
  (Although she then had not believed it)
Her own fair, joyous self, and all
  With whom we were when I received it.
'Tis but a faded flow'r you see,
  Its bloom and beauty all departed,
But may the one who gave it me
  Be always bright and happy-hearted.

ON A PICTURE.

A CALM, sweet face it is, I ween,
 In outlines faultless, perfect quite,
As lovely as it is serene,
 And eyes as beautiful as bright;
She seems in placid, pleasing thought,
 Her mind exempt from every care,
And artist has expression caught
 That shows her as azalea fair.

Her bright brown eyes with beauty glow,
 And even on this card I hold
A radiance rich and sparkling show;
 And worlds of feeling they unfold.
They, too, intelligence proclaim,
 Upreaching to the highest goal,
And something else I need not name,
 For eyes are "windows of the soul."

And then, above those beauteous eyes,
 Harmonious with the eyes themselves
A brow where meditation lies
 Serenely on its polished shelves.
And lips,—ah! how describe those lips!
 Each seems like sweetly budding rose,
From which the bee in summer sips
 The dews from which the honey flows.

A face in every part complete,
　Where beauty's court is all supreme;
A face as noble as 'tis sweet,
　An artist's model, poet's dream.
And though she's far away to-night,
　And may, perhaps, be never near,
Her beauties all are beaming bright,
　And I behold them pictured here.

Heaven bless her in her far-off home,
　And smile upon her from above,
And when the time to her shall come
　(As come it will) that she shall love,
Oh! may the one who wins her heart,
　And love's soft glances from her eyes,
Feel earth has not her counterpart,
　And worthy be of such a prize.

LITTLE PAULINE.

'Twas down at Dixon's Springs we met,
　A summer day not long ago,
And mem'ry will recur, sweet pet,
　To that first meeting oft, I know;
Thy prattling voice I'll often hear,
　Thy bright brown eyes I'll often see,
And in my dreams thou wilt appear
　With kisses and sweet smiles for me.

Reflections may anon be sad,
   And painful recollections bring,
Yet those which wounded deepest had
   An antidote for every sting;
But thou, Pauline, with childish wiles
   And winsome words of love, each day,
Inwreathed in bright and sunny smiles,
   Didst lure my saddened thoughts away.

Though others may have been unkind,
   But few indeed were so to me,
And never, sweet one, did I find
   A symptom of a change in thee;
Pure as the icicle that hung
   On Dian's Temple far away,
Thy heart was loving, and thy tongue
   Had always something sweet to say.

Thy mamma, "papa I I,"* too,
   Were even more than kind to me,
And mem'ry will to them be true,
   As 'twill, sweet little pet, to thee;
When far apart and years roll by,
   Fond recollection shall recall,
With many a tear and many a sigh,
   The faces and the forms of all.

I may perhaps forget a foe,
   Can bear the ills that fortune sends,
Nor murmur 'neath a load of woe,
   But ne'er can I forget my friends;

---

* This is what she calls her grandfather.

Whatever be my faults, Pauline,
    And they perhaps have not been few,
The eye of heaven ne'er has seen
    An act of mine to friend untrue.

The darkened mem'ries! let them go,
    And let me cherish only those
That softly and serenely flow,
    To calm and sweeten my repose;
And in those mem'ries, gentle child,
    Wherever here on earth I be,
In crowded halls, or forest wild,
    Or all alone, I'll cherish thee.

Thy years are few, and yet to come
    To thee are many years and days,
To gladden hearts and brighten home
    With thy sweet, charming, childish ways;
May all those days and all those years
    Be ever bright, Pauline, to thee,
Thine eyes be never dimmed with tears,
    And mayst thou happy ever be.

My aching heart will ere long feel
    Life's bitter pains and pangs no more,
And all its wounds, thank God, will heal
    When life's dark, dismal dream is o'er;
Yet when my skies the darkest be,
    And I the dregs of woe must drink,
'Twill then, I know, be sweet to me
    Of thee, sweet, bright-eyed child, to think.

Assurance sweet I have from thee,
   A place in mem'ry not to grudge,
For, Pauline, thou hast promised me
   That thou wilt ne'er forget " the Judge."
Remember me while yet I live,
   And when the willows o'er me wave,
Still, then, a place in mem'ry give,
   And drop a tear upon my grave.

THE FLOOD.*

Onward, onward, splashing, splashing,
Madly, turbulently dashing,—
Now the sun-rays on them flashing,—
   Wildly on the waters roll;
Mocking feeble man's endeavor,
Angry, restless, pausing never,
Sweeping on and onward ever,
   Scorning guidance and control.

Southward, for the ocean heading,
Yet around us widely spreading,—
Ah! what tears the poor are shedding
   O'er the ruin here and there!
Standing here I gaze and ponder,
See around me, and off yonder,
Far away as eye can wander,
   " Water, water everywhere."

---

* Written during the flood of 1884 in the Ohio River.

Water-fowl above us flying,
Yonder, gallant steamers plying
Hither, thither, bravely trying
    Help to render those who need;
Homes deserted (large and roomy),
Cots and cabins, all now gloomy,
Everything seems dark and doomy,
    Wreck and ruin, sad indeed!

Yesterday, no promise bore us,
Dark and thick the skies hung o'er us,
Darker still the scene before us,
    Dark the prospect, dark the day;
Thrice ten thousand hearts were bleeding
While the flood, no sorrow heeding,
Mocked distress and onward speeding,
    Banished ling'ring hope away.

Wide the spread of devastation,
Ruin holds the situation,
Ruin, ruin, desolation,
    While the wind on every breath
Brings to-day, and will to-morrow,
Tidings full of bitter sorrow,—
Ay, of deep heart-rending sorrow,—
    Hunger, suffering, and death.

Oh! thou Mighty One who knoweth
All that cometh, all that goeth,
Wise and good in all thou doeth,
    Speak and stay the angry tide.

Speak the word, distress relieving,
Speak and soothe the sore and grieving,
From impending death retrieving,
  Bid the raging flood subside.

Look upon thy footstool, Father!
Not in wrath, but mercy rather,
See the homeless suff'rers gather,
  'Reft of shelter and of bread;
Let the sun which now is shining,
Cheerful light and warmth combining,
Show indeed "a silver lining,"
  Hope restore and banish dread.

EPISTLE TO A YOUNG FRIEND.

DEAR Jack, I feel inclined to write
  To you a friendly letter,
Which you may read some wintry night,
  When having nothing better.
I know, while you are far away,
  Your Greek and Latin learning,
Your thoughts will almost every day
  Back here be fondly turning;
For howe'er bright the scenes appear
  By which you are surrounded,
You'll ne'er forget that love has here,
  For you, through life abounded.

You'll find it nowhere else, dear Jack,
    So true, so change-defying;
For though you'll meet with love, 'twill lack
    The principle undying.

The world is full of pits and snares,
    Of evils and of dangers,
And life, my friend, is full of cares,
    Especially 'mong strangers;
For though anon you win a smile,—
    And proud may be to win it,—
Perhaps you, in a little while,
    Will find there's nothing in it.
If friends you find who vary not,
    Don't be too free to use them;
Be frank and candid with them, but,
    Be careful not to lose them.
For some you'll find, who seem your friends,
    Are but like fiery flashes,
A sudden blaze that quickly ends,
    Alone, in smoke and ashes.

Yet don't, for such, mistrust mankind,
    For some are true and trustful,
Though many more, as you will find,
    With selfishness are lustful;
But poisonous weeds grow rank and high
    In nature's fairest bowers,
And often are surrounded by
    The rarest, sweetest flowers.

I've seen, dear Jack, both sides of life,
  Its poverty, its treasures,
Its smiles and frowns, its peace and strife,
  Its sorrows and its pleasures.
I've heard anon the siren's songs,
  Been loved, perhaps, and hated,
I've kindness known and suffered wrongs,
  And think I've graduated.

Life's sky's not always bright, my boy,
  And you must not expect it;
The current gold contains alloy,
  Though you may not detect it.
With honor as your guide, you can
  Meet foes with proud defiance,
And nothing is more noble than
  A manly self-reliance.
The world will back you in success,
  And laud your every action,
But failure and, too oft, distress
  Will dissipate attraction.
Be to yourself and honor true,
  Be proudly independent,
And then, whatever foes may do,
  You'll be in the ascendant.

Dame Fortune's smiles you well may crave,
  And proper homage render,
But never be her cringing slave
  Nor self-respect surrender.

You may not scorn her shining pelf,—
    Attractions are about it,—
But, rather than degrade yourself,
    I know you'll do without it.
Should Cupid aim his polished dart,
    Be brave and do not fear it;
And if it penetrate your heart,
    Don't flinch, my boy, but bear it
(For Cupid will not do you wrong,
    Although a wily sinner),
And when the maiden comes along,
    By manly courtship win her.

The fickle world may frown or smile,
    And men may hate or love you,
But be you ne'er despondent while
    The sunlight beams above you.
Be brave in spirit, strong in heart,
    To meet whate'er await you,
And act a noble, manly part,
    Though hypocrites may hate you.
You may, with conscious pride, look back,
    And be excused for knowing
The blood of noble stock, dear Jack,
    In all your veins is flowing;
And if, with sycophantic smiles,
    The artful seek to win you
From rectitude, repel their wiles,
    And show the manhood in you.

And now, dear Jack, I'll say adieu;
  And I had not intended
To write so lengthily, and you
  Will glad be when I've ended.
Perhaps my letter'll feed the flames
  For hindering your learning,
But it deserves, my friend, and claims
  A better fate than burning.
'Tis prompted by a motive pure,—
  True friendship, don't forget it,—
And if you'll ponder it, I'm sure
  That you will not regret it.
But now adieu, bright, noble boy;
  May sorrow touch you never;
May peace, prosperity, and joy
  Be yours, dear Jack, forever.

NO HEART CONCEALMENTS.

"You must not give your feelings vent,"
  So said a friend one day.
I have no doubt my good was meant,
  But I've a word to say:
I may not be, perhaps, as wise
  As was the one who spoke,
Yet I from sympathetic eyes
  Would not my feelings cloak.

One must give vent to feelings when
    They come of joy or grief;
It multiplies the first by ten,
    And brings the last relief;
For pent-up joy, like miser's gold,
    Brings never aught of gain,
While hoarded griefs will, many a fold,
    Increase the bitter pain.

The heart was never made to be
    Like wood or stone or steel,
But sensitive to touch, and free
    A joy or pain to feel;
Its joy it lets the loving know,
    Thus both to vivify,
And if it broods on untold woe,
    'Twill surely droop and die.

Neith'r joys nor sorrows may be pent,
    Like animals of prey;
'Tis always best to give them vent,
    No matter which are they;
Unless to some a wrong 'twould do
    To bare the heart and mind,
And then 'twere better, wiser too,
    To keep the thoughts confined.

Ah! sympathy is very sweet,
    As fate to me has shown,
But this we cannot hope to meet,
    Unless its want is known;

And if with friends to help us bear
  Life's ills their pain destroys,
It pleasure will enhance to share
  With them our purest joys.

And I—it may be I am wrong,
  But so I ne'er have thought—
Have never, as I jogged along,
  My heart concealment taught;
I never could—nor sought to—hide
  My pleasures or my woes
From friends in whom I might confide,
  Nor even from my foes.

And so, thus far, I've run my race,
  My kind, unselfish friend,
And so will jog along apace
  Until I reach the end,
Appreciating none the less
  The kind advice you give;
And you I pray that heav'n may bless
  And smile on while you live.

MY LIFE IS LIKE AN APRIL SKY.

My life is like an April sky,
  By floating clouds anon o'ercast,
And then illuminated by
  Soft sun-rays when the clouds have passed;

And when the shades of night shall come
Across the erewhile gilded dome,
That sky shall still remembered be,
But none will ever think of me.

My life is like the fickle breeze
  That sometimes whistles swiftly by,
Then lingers softly 'mong the trees,
  To murmur sadly there and sigh;
    And when the summer's sun shall glow,
    And then no more those breezes blow,
    Their absence shall awake regret,
    But all, alas! will me forget.

My life is like the sunny beams
  That sometimes sky and earth illume,
Yet oft, when promise brightest seems,
  Are hid away by clouds and gloom;
    And when those beams are all withdrawn,
    And every ray of sunlight gone,
    We sigh o'er nature's stern decree,
    But none, alas! will sigh for me.

My life is like the skylark's notes,
  As upward he, on buoyant wings,
Soars heavenward, and the nearer floats
  To Paradise the sweeter sings;
    And when he to the earth descends
    His song in all its sweetness ends,
    That song shall still remembered be,
    But none will think again of me.

THE BANKER'S BOY.

The banker has a noble boy,—
   A nobler one is not alive,—
His papa's pride, his mamma's joy,
   And on the roll he's Number Five.
No boy the banker's boy outranks,
   And, like a petted only son,
He perpetrates his boyish pranks,
   But this he always does in fun.

He's hardly two years old to-day,
   Nor is he more than two feet high,
But he will be, I dare to say,
   A great big fellow by and by.
There's spirit quite enough in him
   To all his energies employ,
And there is "lots and cords" o' vim
   And genius in that banker's boy.

His taste is exquisite in buds,
   Both out of doors and in the room,
And morn and eve away he scuds
   To find the rarest one in bloom.
Sweet Calla lilies are his choice,
   And, for a button-hole bouquet,
To make his boyish heart rejoice,
   He plucked his mamma's last one day.

He's fond of fun, that banker's boy,
    But puts old notions on the shelf,
Prefers his genius to employ
    In planning fun to suit himself;
And if, whene'er his plans are ripe,
    He spies a kitten round about,
He stuffs it down the sewer-pipe,
    And leaves mamma to pull it out.

A carriage is that boy's delight;
    Not that he cares a whit to ride,
But watches it in rapid flight,
    And laughs to see it swiftly glide;
And if in sunshine, without hat,
    He starts it on a breakneck run,
Suppose it smashes, what of that?
    The banker's boy must have his fun.

And if he takes his mamma's shoe
    To dip the water from a pan,
What could that doting mamma do
    But kiss and pet the little man?
And papa's hat a useful thing
    He finds, when pies of clay he'd make,
The water and the clay to bring,
    The pies to form for sun to bake.

That boy, I'm sure, is bound to be
    The greatest man the country knows,
And though somewhat mischievous, he
    Will drop his mischief as he grows;

So here I toast the banker's boy :
Long may he live and ever thrive,
Be papa's pride and mamma's joy,
Though on the roll as Number Five.

ALAS! TOO LATE!

Suggested by, and responsive to, " Coming Home at Last," by Will Carleton, in " Harper's Weekly."*

THE exile was, indeed, too long,
  And sad the wand'ring poet's fate,
The whole wide world had sung his song,
  But offered him a home too late;
Although for this he long had pined,
  And with the years those pinings grew,
Within his noble heart was shrined
  That which, alas! he never knew;
Yet he had roamed from place to place,
  Till, far away on Afric's strand,
He fell asleep in death's embrace,
  A stranger in a stranger's land.

There was a time when gentle voice
  Had lightly caused his blood to speed,
And made his aching heart rejoice ;
  But that was in his time of need ;

---

* The removal of the remains of John Howard Payne, the author of " Home, Sweet Home," from his African to an American grave.

Then, as he strolled o'er hill and plain,
    He gazed with longing, wistful eye
In search of that, alas! in vain,
    Which could his heart's one want supply;
He plodded on, and heard his song
    Resounding sweetly everywhere,
Yet found no place his road along
    That he was not a stranger there.

No, no; we see no "cheerful brow,"
    No step bespeaking "conscious pride;"
For all is dust and ashes now,
    And homeless and alone he died.
There was a time he might have been
    Made happy by a helping hand,
And those who helped him might have seen
    His heart with gratitude expand;
But now, alas! that heart is cold,
    No longer feels the grateful breath,
And neither pæans, love, nor gold
    Can "soothe the dull, cold ear of death."

Ah, yes! he "thrilled the world with song,"
    Made every pulse more quickly move,
And filled the hearts of every throng
    With sympathy and tender love;
And as he plodded on apace
    His weary, long, and lonesome track,
He scattered blessings on his race,
    But, ah! received no blessing back.

He brightened every home, but, sad
  To think, alas! he died alone
Upon a foreign shore, and had
  No home that he could call his own.

His song the hearts of men had thrilled,
  Perchance those hearts more tender made,
Into them deeper love instilled,
  And all with gentle power swayed;
And yet, sweet singer though he was,
  And taught mankind the worth of home,
Despite the world's unsought applause,
  He lived, alas! alone to roam;
And though a home is his at last
  In Freedom's land, yet cruel fate
Withheld it till his dream had passed,
  And now it is too late, too late!

But let us hope that he who could
  Cause hearts the charms of home to know,
Sway here the cold and rude for good,
  Has found a "Sweet Home" long ago;
That he who human souls could fill
  With that divine emotion, love,
Heard angel-voices sweetly trill,
  Inviting to a home above;
And let us hope in that bright land,
  All fragrant, beautiful, and fair,
Among the bless'd immortal band
  He has a home eternal there.

"OH, EVER THUS!"

To bear the brunt of toil and strife,
    Feel sorrow's deep consuming pain,
And see the dearest ties of life
    Like brittle threads all snapt in twain;
To know that frowns upon you rest,
    That eretime words are all forgot,
To clasp the arrow to your breast,
    Perhaps is but the common lot.

Yet there are hearts so finely strung,
    So sensitive to eye's cold glance;
So true, that though they suffer long
    And deeply feel the poisoned lance,
They cannot cover nor disguise,
    Although they gladly would conceal—
Conceal at least from loved ones' eyes—
    The bitter anguish that they feel.

"Oh, ever thus!" so poet sung,
    Yet not alone *his* heart has felt
The cruel shaft by coldness flung,
    And seen its brightest visions melt;
For there are living those to-day
    For whom life once was fair and bright,
But now is dark, with not a ray
    To soften down the gloom of night.

They loved; oh, with that holy faith!
   Devotion gave with childlike trust,
Till perished hope in icy death,
   When love was trampled in the dust.
They bore the torture fortune sent,
   They bear it still, and only crave
That soon may all its force be spent,
   And rest be found within the grave.

Bear up awhile, ye stricken souls,
   Nor yield to cold unfeeling blows,
A higher pow'r your fate controls,
   And He your truth and sorrow knows;
Though coldness may the heart congeal,
   When frowns the cherished brows o'ercast,
The anguish that is yours conceal,
   And hope for solace sweet at last.

TO LITTLE GRETCHEN.

Gentle lassie, smiling ever,
   And with bright and open brow,
'Tis my prayer that thou shalt never
   Be less free from care than now;
Heaven guard thee from all sadness,
   Every sorrow, every pain,
Fill thy heart with joy and gladness,
   There forever to remain.

Childhood's pleasures are abounding,
    Full of innocence and love,
Bright all scenes thy life surrounding,
    Bright the skies that hang above;
Thus may ever, 'round and o'er thee,
    Peace and happiness entwine,
Flowers deck the way before thee,
    Planted by the hand Divine.

Like a ray of sunlight, streaming
    Down from yonder skies above,
Comes thy smile, sweet lassie, beaming
    Bright with hope, and joy, and love;
Oh! may shadow ne'er conceal it,
    Sorrow never drive away,
Cold misfortune ne'er congeal it,
    But, may it still beam for aye.

May thy life be one of gladness,
    One of peace, content, and joy,
Free from pain and care and sadness,—
    Gold indeed without alloy:—
And, whene'er its dream is ended,
    And its peaceful voyage o'er,
Then with pleasures be it blended
    On sweet Adenne's flow'ry shore.

When I, silently, am sleeping,
    And the vines above me wave,
Where the swaying willow, weeping,
    Marks my cold and lonely grave,

Then, when cares no more beset me,
 And life's weary work is past,
Think of, and do not forget, me,
 Gentle Gretchen, to the last.

FIRST SNOW.

WINTER blasts are blowing bleakly,
 Wildly swaying vine and tree,
Dashing on with shriek and whistle,
 In a weird-like minstrelsy;
And, like phantoms, as if dancing
 To the music of despair,
Waltzing round and round, and whirling,
 Snow-flakes thickly fill the air.

On the lawn no sunlight sparkles,
 Spreading there a genial glow,
And the verdure yet remaining
 Disappears beneath the snow;
All without is cold and cheerless,
 Dreary to the mind and eye,
Yet my heart is feeling grateful
 As the bleak winds whistle by.

Here I sit in warmth and comfort,
 And my grate is glowing bright,
While I see out through the window
 Snow-flakes flying cold and white;

Cold and white and all unfeeling,
   Heedless where they fall or lay,
Heedless of the poor who shiver
   In the cutting winds to-day.

And as evening shadows gather,
   Colder still and sharper blow,
Through the trees, the blasts of winter,
   And the faster falls the snow.
Ah! when night has spread its mantle
   O'er the earth and hid from view
All the dreary scenes out yonder,
   What will then the homeless do?

Nay, say not the homeless only,
   For too many homes there are
With but stinted bread and shelter,
   And no earthly comfort there.
'Round a few fast-dying embers
   There will huddle through the night
Many a shiv'ring babe and mother,
   Praying for the morning light.

And, while I and mine shall slumber,
   Dreaming darkness all away,
Ah! how many will be sleepless,
   Watching, longing for the day!
God have mercy on the needy!
   While the bitter tempests blow,
Give them comfort and protection
   From the cold, the sleet, and snow.

DREAMS WILL VANISH! HOPES WILL PERISH!

STRANGE, that sweetest dreams will vanish
  When most dear to heart and eye;
Yet a chilly breeze will banish
  Warmth and glow from earth and sky;
Dreams are fancy's figments only,
  Yet there's many a loving heart
Which will feel forlorn and lonely
  When their ling'ring shades depart;
Many a heart sincere and tender,
  Honest, faithful, steadfast, true,
Would ev'n life itself surrender
  Rather than its dreams forego.
It may be that vain presumption
  Buoys the heart and spirit up,
And perhaps a wild assumption
  Fills that heart with baseless hope,
But 'twill go on vainly dreaming,
  Till hope's star withdraws its light,
Then, when not a ray is gleaming,
  All will vanish in the night.

Strange, that fondest hopes will perish
  Ev'n when faith is soaring high,
Yet the sweetest flow'r we cherish
  In the wintry blast will die.

Hope is like a bird or flower
  Nurtured by a loving hand,
If neglected, in some hour,
  These will die, and that will strand;
Strand and wreck, alas! forever,
  Crushed by coldness and disdain,
Sink into despair, and never
  Be revived to life again.
Then, while consciousness shall linger,
  Grief will pierce like pois'nous thorn,
While hope's ghost, with mocking finger,
  Points at misery in scorn.
Death seems then too slow in coming,
  Though we pray for his approach,
Till some morn, or noon, or gloaming,
  He relieves us by his touch.

Strange, how loving hearts will languish
  When their cold death-wounds are giv'n,
Yet the dart which gives most anguish
  By the dearest hand is driv'n.
Love will always furnish fuel
  For the flame 'twould keep alive,
But indifference, or cruel
  Coldness, it can ne'er survive:
It may live ev'n though rejected,
  For it feeds upon its own,
But 'twill die if 'tis neglected,
  After being smiled upon.

Kinder far to send the arrow
  Where 'twill stop the fleeting breath,
Than entail consuming sorrow
  Which will bring slow, ling'ring death.
Dreams have vanished, hopes have perished,
  Hearts have languished too, yet I
Cling to hopes that I have cherished;
  When I yield them I would die.

THE SNOW AND THE CHILDREN.

SWIFTLY down the snow is drifting
  From the cold and sunless sky,
O'er the earth a carpet spreading
  Where the fleecy atoms lie.
Carpet? No, 'twere far more fitting,
  Though 'tis trampled 'neath our feet,
Thing so dismal, cold and ghostly,
  Bear the name of winding-sheet.

As I faced the blast this morning,
  Snow-flakes falling thick and fast,
Happy children, bright and smiling,
  Voiced their pleasure as they passed.
Happy children, full of gladness,
  Full of joy the snow to see,
Guileless, free from care and sadness,
  As should childhood ever be.

When I met them memory told me,
  As I looked on each bright brow,
Once was I as gay and joyous
  As are these sweet children now.
Once as glad, in dreary winter,
  As are they to see the snow,
Just as sportive and as happy,—
  Ah! but that was long ago.

Then my locks, like raven's plumage,
  Typified more night and day,
Now the snow that taps them gently
  Hardly whiter is than they.
Then my step was light and buoyant,
  And my eyes with brightness shone,
Now that step is slow and halting,
  And from eyes that lustre's gone.

Many winters have passed o'er me,
  Ices, winds, and snow, and all,
And I've wept o'er many a loved one
  I have seen around me fall.
Ah, I have seen them, like the snow-flakes,
  Which now spread the pavement o'er,
Even as they tossed and struggled,
  Fall, alas! to rise no more.

Happy children, who out yonder
  Met me but awhile ago,
Let them in their own bright spring-time
  Greet with glee the winter's snow.

Not a flake around them falling
  On this sunless Sabbath-day,
Though it from the heavens drifted,
  Freer is from stain than they.

May they, when the threads of silver
  Streak their tresses by and by,
Or when snow their brows is crowning,
  And they older are than I,
Be then, as they now are, able,
  Sinless hearts and lives to show,
Consciences as free from blemish
  And as stainless as the snow.

A CHILD'S PICTURE.

AH! how mem'ry's waves break o'er me,
  As I sit and gaze the while
On this sweet young face before me,
  Giving back a smile for smile!
How it brings life's rosy morning
  Back to view, with all its scenes,
When I watched fair hands adorning
  Here and yonder May-day queens!
Some were yet in budding childhood,
  Others older, all were fair,
And from garden, field, and wildwood
  Garlands decked their flowing hair.

Since these days the weeping-willows
   Over some their shades have spread,
Where they slumber, earth their pillows,
   And to each a lonely bed.
Others live in life's calm autumn,
   Looking forth to wintry age,
Cold experience having taught 'em
   Life's book has but one bright page;
That one page is decked with flowers
   Drinking sunlight from above,
Beautifying vernal bowers,
   Fragrant with the breath of love.

Maiden, on whose face I'm gazing,
   In whose sparkling eyes, I ween,
Bright intelligence is blazing,
   Though so placid and serene,
Life's bright pathway lies before thee,
   Sunlight now thy sky adorns;
May no storm-cloud e'er loom o'er thee,
   Nor thy path be marred with thorns,
May kind heaven guide and guard thee
   Till life's dangers all are past,
And when toil is o'er, reward thee
   With eternal bliss at last.

DO I LOVE SOLITUDE?

Do I (you ask) love solitude?
    Fair lady, that depends
Much on my temper and my mood,
    Or on what fortune sends.
I've drank her smiles and felt her frowns,
    Have good received and ill;
For years have borne life's "ups and downs,"
    And these am bearing still;
And when my heart is light and glad
    I'd have my gladness known,
But when I'm "out o' sorts" and sad,
    I want to be alone.

I cannot say I'm overfond
    Of being by myself,
Or sinking into deep despond,
    Or lying on a shelf.
Whatever good the world can give,
    I like to have my share,
And while I live, I want to live,
    And laugh at grim despair.
I like to have *true* friends around,
    Too few they are, alas!
The false and fickle more abound,
    But these may "go to grass."

No bachelor, fair friend, am I,
  All covered o'er with crust,
And you may bet I'll never die
  From idleness or rust.
Some dangers, now and then, I've dared,
  But I have never known
The time in life I would have cared
  To "go it all alone."
I think I'd lose all self-respect,
  Feel something like a hog,
If I could social joys reject
  For life within a log.

So you, and all my fair young friends
  (And these I hope aren't few),
Will see that very much depends
  On what the fates may do
To buoy me up or press me down,
  To make me laugh or groan,
Wheth'r (as they wear a smile or frown)
  I'd rather be alone;
But if I must, unlike most men,
  Trim down my answer fine,
Responding "yea" or "nay," why, then,
  No solitude in mine.

LORENA IN TEARS.

AH! tears bespeak a tender heart,
  And sometimes when I see them flow,
My own, unbidden, too, will start,
  As if 'twere mine to share the woe;
Nor envy I the callous soul,
  Though wrapt and revelling in weal,
Which cannot tenderly condole
  With friends, and for their sorrows feel.

I saw a fair, sweet face one day,
  On which before had only shone
Bright smiles that chased all care away,
  And haven seemed for these alone;
A face where innocence is seen
  In every dimple, every line,
Bespeaking conscience all serene,
  And soul that tender thoughts enshrine.

I saw it when like beaming sun,
  Bespangling rain-drops as they fell,
'Twas touching sweet to gaze upon,
  Through crystals from the heart's deep well;
It told me in its soft repose
  The heart, whence came those tears, was true,
Reminded me of blushing rose,
  Or pure, sweet lily bathed in dew.

Ah! tears are sweet, and even though grief
    Provoke them from the soul to rise,
Yet to that soul they give relief,
    When brimming from the soft bright eyes;
And I should doubt the purest heart,
    And doubt its power life to bless,
Whence bright, warm tears could never start
    At voice of sorrow and distress.

I know the heart is ever right,
    And pure as flake of falling snow,
When from the gentle eyes, and bright,
    I see the sparkling tear-drops flow.
And thine, fair one, I thus have read;
    I know that virtue nestles there,
And pray that thou mayst never shed
    One tear-drop wrenched by cold despair.

MY MOUSEY VISITOR.

I've sometimes sat in solitude,
    To gloomy thoughts a prey,
In silent contemplative mood,—
    My loved ones far away,—
And felt my Cozy Nook would be
    Less like a charnel-house
If I, anon, could even see
    A tiny little mouse.

And I have sat alone at night,
  And wished that one would come,
And thought I'd give him, with delight,
  A welcome to my room.
I'd show him that he had a friend
  Who was "a friend indeed,"
And one on whom he might depend
  For crumbs, on which to feed.

Well, last night, while alone I sat,—
  Exchanges looking o'er,
In solitude, and feeling that
  It was a gloomy bore,—
I looked down on the hearth by chance,
  The well-filled grate ablaze,
And there, responsive to my glance,
  A mousey met my gaze.

He shyly glanced at me awhile,—
  The gaslight brightly glared,—
And mousey must have seen me smile,
  For he did not seem scared.
I wished that I had then at hand
  Some tempting morsel near,
With which to make him understand
  How welcome he was here.

I gently rose and looked around
  For something that would please
My mousey, and at last I found
  A little piece of cheese.

I laid it where I thought he'd go,
    And though it was quite small,
I hoped he'd be content, to know
    I'd given him my all.

The little fellow soon came out,
    And eyed me as before,
Then eyed the cheese, and I've no doubt
    He "sorrow'd 'twas no more."
But I of even this was glad,
    And hoped my mouse would stay,
But seizing it,—though all I had,—
    He scampered right away.

And mousey is but like—I thought—
    False friends we all have known,
Who, when shall vanish all we've got,
    Will leave us then, alone;
But whene'er fortune on us rain
    Its smiles, they strive to please,
As mousey 'll surely come again
    When I have got more cheese.

THE BEAUTIFUL TRIO.

In a neat little town on the lower Ohio
    I saw, not a great while ago,
A joyous and blooming and beautiful trio,
    As charming as any I know.

Quite petite were all, neither weighed over eighty,
   Symmetrical, graceful, and neat,—
None more so than Flora, and Effie, and Katie,
   And gentle they as they were sweet.

Though flowers, down there, in the gardens were blooming,
   The eye, mind, and heart all to please,
Each breeze and each soft, floating zephyr perfuming,
   Yet none were more lovely than these.

The largest perhaps of the trio was Flora,
   And sweet little Effie the least,
And each was as fair and as bright as Aurora
   When, rose-crowned, she smiles in the east.

I met the bright triplet, first one, then another,
   But somehow I did not once see
The beautiful bouquet all blended together,
   Though several times saw I all three.

And oft have I thought of them since we have parted,
   Will so think again and again,
And wish that they always may be happy-hearted,
   And never know sorrow nor pain.

Too young and too innocent trouble to borrow,
   May naught ever mar their repose,
As now, in their innocence, strangers to sorrow,
   So may it be down to life's close.

May friends be not lacking to smile on them ever,
  And sweet acts of friendliness do,
And those whom they love, and are dear to them, never
  Be fickle, unkind, or untrue.

Heav'n spare them the coldness that heart's love estranges,
  God bless them, each one and all three,
And save them from that sort of friendship which changes
  Whenever convenient it be.

The dear, charming, beautiful, innocent trio,
  All living so far, far away,
In fair "Conda" town on the lower Ohio,
  May heaven smile on them for aye.

My muse sings this morning—the dawn of September—
  Her first autumn song to the three,
And asks that each dear little friend will remember,
  And kindly think sometimes of me.

POETRY.

(Dedicated to Mrs. E. L. S.)

The volumes beautifully wrought,
  And filled, in figures clear and bold,
With gems of purest virgin thought,
  All bound in "Russia" and in gold,

We know, in glowing words, contain
   That which they say is born above,
Creations of the poet's brain,
   Outpourings of the poet's love.

And this is poetry they say;
   Perhaps it is, and yet methinks
My eager, thirsting soul each day,
   From myriads of fountains, drinks
A sweeter poetry than e'er
   Is found in volumes, though they be
As bright as star-decked skies appear,
   Or rich as gems beneath the sea.

It floats upon the balmy breeze,
   Expands in beauty o'er the skies,
It drips like rain-drops from the trees,
   And softly beams in woman's eyes;
'Tis seen in tints of every bloom
   That beautifies the fruitful earth,
It sanctifies and softens gloom,
   And purity imparts to mirth.

'Tis heard in every thunder-crash
   That startles slumb'ring nature, and
'Tis seen in every lightning-flash
   Shot forth by Jove's resistless hand;
'Tis heard in song of every bird
   That nature's anthems sweetly sings,
'Tis everywhere, and seen and heard
   In twice ten thousand, thousand things.

'Tis God's own way to show His love,
    And make the saddened soul rejoice;
He speaks it from His throne above,—
    For poetry is love's own voice.
Its mission is to elevate
    The thoughts, and these to purify,
The heart's warm love to concentrate
    On what is worthy, pure, and high.

Ah me! how I have longed to strike
    The tuneful lyre, and hear it trill
Upon the breeze, its music like
    To that which heav'nly bodies thrill!
How I have vainly longed to mount
    Parnassus, where the muses, first
In waters of Castalian fount,
    Assuaged ambition's eager thirst!

I drink the draughts I catch below,
    But these, alas! can only serve
The vainness of my hopes to show,
    And yet my fainting soul they nerve;
And as I drain each sparkling cup
    My eager gaze I upward cast,
Then soar my aspirations up,
    In hope to reach the fount at last.

Thou, lady, hast my soul inspired
    With courage still to struggle on,
Anew hath my ambition fired
    When this and hope were wellnigh gone;

Thy kindly words have given me
　　Fresh inspiration, stronger zeal;
For this I grateful am to thee,
　　And here my longings all reveal.

Perhaps we here shall meet no more,
　　But where the fragrant air resounds
With music on the other shore,
　　Where purest poetry abounds,
Up yonder 'mong the blessed above,
　　When life's uncertain dream is o'er,
May thou and I, and all we love,
　　Together meet to part no more.

PARTED.

They loved as few had ever loved,
　　Though once perhaps, awhile, estranged,
But heart-devotion potent proved,
　　And vows eternal were exchanged;
He drank the nectar from her lips,
　　Received and gave love's ling'ring kiss;
They pledged that naught should e'er eclipse
　　Their visions of eternal bliss.

Sweet words were spoken: they had found
　　A heaven here on earth below;
Their hearts, by golden cords, were bound
　　In ties that could no parting know.

One promise only did he crave,
    To paint with rosy tints his skies,
And this confidingly she gave,
    While love and hope illumed her eyes.

She promised she would bear his name,
    That nothing should her love subdue;
Though clouds and storms and sorrows came,
    To him she'd be forever true.
He pressed her fondly to his side,
    Again their lips in raptures met;
She pledged herself to be his bride,—
    That pledge he hoped she'd ne'er forget.

His soul with deep devotion burned;
    She bade him patient be and brave,
That tenfold she the love returned
    Which he to her so fondly gave;
She said her heart should never range
    From his, but that their love should blend
Together, and she ne'er would change,
    But true remain until life's end.

Ah, yes! they loved each other then,—
    He thought *she* loved, and *he* adored,
Nor dreamed he time was coming when
    Revoked would be each loving word.
His hope and trust were sweet and strong;
    He spurned the thought that one so pure,
And lovable, could do a wrong,
    And love's allegiance abjure.

Alas! while thus he lived in bliss,
  And fondly nursed the glowing flame,—
Each glance, each word, each loving kiss,—
  The change, all unexpected, came.
She calmly told him all was o'er,
  And coldly cancelled every vow,
She bade him cherish hope no more,
  And they, alas! are parted now.

And this is life,—nay, this is fate,—
  Deep, earnest love and faith are giv'n,
Till wakened from the dream too late,
  By cold despair the heart is riv'n.
And when from blissful dreams it wakes,
  Which full of joy and promise seemed,
The tortured heart bears, bleeds, and breaks,
  To find how vainly it had dreamed.

OH, YES, I'M JOLLY (?).

"I hope you are your jolly self again."—*Extract from a friendly letter.*

Oh, yes, I am my jolly self,
  As every one can plainly see;
I've laid the blues upon the shelf,
  And sickness now don't trouble me.

I'm not as when you saw me last,
    Though frosty still remains my hair,
But I am fatt'ning up so fast
    That I will rival soon a bear.

I ate but little, as you saw,—
    I simply slept, and smoked, and wrote,—
But now I think that I could "chaw"
    The horns off any Billy-goat.
I "hanker" not for these, 'tis true;
    I'd rather have an oyster-pie,
A roast, a scallop, broil, or stew,
    Or ev'n a neatly breaded fry.

But, then, I take whate'er I get,
    And never in my stomach find
A squeamish tendency to fret,
    But "jollily" I "go it blind."
Your mamma bade me once beware
    Of devils blue, and shun them all;
They used to, but now never dare
    To sport or flirt with me at all.

My "jolly self!" Well, you may bet
    Against the pile of Uncle Sam,
That free from mopings, ne'er a fret,
    That's just precisely what I am.
Like Moore, I "sigh for those who love,"
    Like him, I "smile for those who hate,"
Like him, "whatever sky's above"
    I have "a heart for every fate."

My conscience suffers not from shocks,
  And now and then I "spin a yarn,"
And my well-worn and "holey" socks
  Alone receive from me a "darn";
I have no grudge against mankind,
  And if my coat or pants I rend,
I sit me down with placid mind,
  And hum a ditty while I mend.

If friends betray I let 'em rip,
  But ne'er myself desert the true;
If bridesmaid offers me "a dip,"
  I tell her "I have gotten through."
Sub rosa, I confess that I,
  One balmy summer evening fine,
Was told that somewhere this reply
  Was made by sweeter lips than mine.

Oh, yes! I am my "jolly self,"—
  At least I, somehow, think I am,—
Enjoying life,—not scorning pelf,—
  And naught about me is a "sham."
I'm taking things just as they come,
  And think that I have wiser grown,—
I ought, for while I've rollicked some,
  I've bitter disappointments known.

But sorrows now I laugh away,
  Expel them all from memory, too,
And if blue devils block my way,
  I kick them out, "you bet" I do.

I'm " fat and forty,"—maybe more,—
And " jolly" as a sportive elf,
Yet fickleness of friends deplore,—
How is it, lady, with yourself?

LIFE'S SHOW.

'Tis said the world is all a show,
    With lots o' fun and folly,
And now and then a cloud of woe
    Or shade of melancholy;
But I have always tried to look
    Upon the side that's brightest,
Though doubtless I've anon mistook
    The blackest for the whitest.
I've laughed at fortune when it frowned,
    And courage tried to borrow
When ghostly phantoms capered round,
    And threatened me with sorrow.
I tried awhile a single life,
    In wholesome fear of rabies,
A fretful and a scolding wife,
    And troops of squalling babies.
Though lone my morns and afternoons,—
    And nights and evenings matched 'em,—
Yet when I tore my pantaloons
    I whistled while I patched 'em.

'Gainst woman's wiles myself I thought
  Too solid to be tackled,
Until one evening I was caught
  And pretty soon was shackled.
They say that woman's weakest, and
  'Tis manly to defend her,
But pretty soon she takes command,
  And strength must then surrender.
I took the noose without a fear
  Of fancy's startling pictures,
For well I knew I'd never hear
  The well-meant curtain lectures.
I felt quite tickled in my mind,
  And fell at once to guessing
How long 'twould be ere I should find
  My deafness was a blessing.

Well, on I went, and rattled up
  Life's rugged mountain, crownward,
Until I reached the snowy top,
  And now I'm looking downward.
The way on which I soon shall pass
  With rocks and thorns is sprinkled,
And I can see, from tell-tale glass,
  I'm gray, but am not wrinkled;
And yet I feel as young to-day
  As when I upward started,
For, though my locks and beard are gray,
  I'm sure I'm not gray-hearted.
I have *some* friends I know are true,—
  I do not know how many,—

But I don't fret that they are few,
   I'm only glad of any;
For well I know—ah! I have seen
   Behind life's flimsy curtain—
Unselfish friends are far between,
   And others are uncertain.
If those I love will ne'er forget
   The love that I am giving,
And full return will make, there's yet
   Some joy for me in living;
And I would rather far believe
   That every one's a jewel
Than think that one would me deceive,
   Or fickle be or cruel.
Then let the show go briskly on,
   With tragedy or drama,
Or farce (for people all like "fun")
   Or moving panorama;
I'll sit and gaze with all the rest,
   Without my mind exertin'
To criticise the worst or best,
   Till down shall drop the curtain.

"YOUR TRUE FRIEND."

How oft these simple words are writ
   (Which should so much convey),
When they but hollow sounds transmit,
   That pass like wind away!

Though sacred when with true intent
    They uttered are, I own,
Yet, when in mere calm compliment,
    They're mockery alone.

A true friend is a friend indeed,
    Who gives no cruel pain,
Nor causes loving hearts to bleed
    That ever true remain.
A true friend never makes a pledge
    Without intent to keep,
Just for the "glorious privilege"
    Of seeing others weep.

A true friend scorns to do a wrong
    Unto a trusting one,
And frowns upon the heartless throng
    Who ridicule in fun;
Not only so, but such a friend
    Will kindness only do,
Defy mutation to the end,
    And steadfast be and true.

The world is full of fickle friends;
    We meet them everywhere;
Their friendship all, we know, depends
    On cloudless skies and fair,
And often, too, upon the use
    Which they of us can make;
And should we one request refuse,
    The ties of friendship break.

I've met them oft from manhood's dawn,
    Have trusted and believed,—
In blind, sweet faith have trusted on,
    To find myself deceived;
And then I've paused a little while
    To retrospect and think
How such could give me, with a smile,
    A cup of woe to drink.

No, no; the words (though sacred they),
    As I myself have seen,
And still am seeing every day,
    Too often nothing mean.
If you'd escape stern memory's frown,
    And "paths of peace" pursue,
Those sacred words no more write down
    Unless you *feel* they're true.

TAKE BACK THOSE WORDS.

"I have just received the sad intelligence of the death of another of my beloved friends.
   *   *   *   *   *   *   *   *
"I pray I may not be left here long to mourn for them."— *Letter from a "friend in sorrow."*

Take back those gloomy words, fair friend,
    They sound not well from such as thou;
A sunny radiance heav'n will send
    To drive all shadows from thy brow;

Nay, more, will send into thy heart
    Ten thousand pleasure-giving beams,
To make all sadness thence depart
    And bless thy life with happy dreams.

Thy heart will soon be glad and gay,
    The skies be bright above thy head,
And flowers bloom along thy way,
    Their fragrance on thy life to shed.
'Tis said that love will cast out fear;
    Why may it not assuage all grief?
'Twill sanctify the pearly tear
    Which flows to give the heart relief.

The world is bright before thee now,
    And brighter it will grow, fair friend,
And, if 'twere mine to order, thou
    Shouldst happy be until life's end;
Nor doubt I that thou wilt be so,—
    I could not doubt it if I would,—
For I, as well as others, know
    That thou art gentle, fair, and good.

What if, perchance, thou hast anon
    A change in thine emotions felt?
What if, perchance, in days now gone,
    Blows cruel thou hast sometimes dealt?
These all by thee were soon forgot,
    And then to sorrow came surcease;
Such things should be remembered not
    If they a moment mar thy peace.

A host of friends all love thee now,
    And this should make reflection sweet,
And lovers for thy smiles will bow
    In adoration at thy feet.
Why shouldst thou court the gloom of night,
    Or think that life will cheerless be,
When every prospect seems so bright,
    Foretelling peace and joy to thee?

No, no; take back those bitter words;
    They'd more befit such lips as mine;
The thought they speak but ill accords
    With natures joyous as is thine.
Drive off the thoughts that crowd thy brain,
    The sadness weighing on thy heart,
Reflections that occasion pain,
    And bid them all for aye depart.

Remember, Him who made thee willed
    That thou thy race of life shouldst run,
Until, thy destiny fulfilled,
    He calls thy name, and says, "Well done."
Do not His call anticipate,
    And, though His ways thou canst not see,
Be sure, fair friend, that, soon or late,
    There's much of happiness for thee.

Thy bright young life must not be marred
    By gloomy, dismal thoughts like these;
They suit alone the battle-scarred,
    Who look to death for rest and ease.

Revoke that prayer for early death,
   Contented, happy be, and know
(For He has said it) "as thy faith"
   So shall life's stream serenely flow.

TO MY WIFE.

You've made a request such as never
   Before you have asked at my hands,
Though all your requests I have ever
   Regarded as loving commands.

You ask me to write you a poem;
   My effort may little avail,
But let me say here, in the proem,
   I'd try, though I knew I should fail.

You very well knew when you asked me
   I'd call, if I could, the coy muse,
For however much it had tasked me,
   I'd not have the heart to refuse.

For well, my dear wife, I remember
   A boon that I asked long ago,—
One dreary and snowy December,—
   Nor heard I such answer as "no."

We've travelled life's pathway together,
   From base to the top of the hill,
In sunshine and cold wintry weather,
   And thus we are journeying still.

The summit passed, we are now going
   Adown the west slope to the plain,
And now and then glance backward, knowing
   We'll ne'er see the hill-top again.

Like others, we've had cares and troubles,
   For life is not all a sweet dream,
And here and there rioting bubbles
   Appear on the most placid stream.

Love's pledges to us have been given,
   And thrice we've been sorely bereft,
But those who have gone are in heaven,
   And still we have three dear ones left.

And dearly and fondly we've loved them,
   The living and those in the grave,
And time has, with every test, proved them
   All worthy the love that we gave.

We've nothing seen baneful nor hateful,
   No blemish of heart to lament,
And we, I am sure, should be grateful
   To heaven for all that it sent.

Though riches ne'er with us abounded,
    For lucre we never could hoard,
Yet comfort and love have surrounded
    "Sweet home," and content crowned the board.

A poem you ask, and I sorrow
    That never my loftiest dream,
Nor aught from the muse I might borrow,
    Could rise to the height of my theme.

Your finger bears on it a token,
    Placed there when you stood by my side,
And words were all solemnly spoken
    Which made you my own blushing bride.

Your tresses were dark then and flowing,
    Your step was elastic and light,
Your soft cheeks with sweet roses glowing,
    Your eyes, as the planets, were bright.

And though years have passed, and time's finger
    Left pencillings others may see,
The beauties of maidenhood linger,
    And you are still lovely to me.

Your eyes, if less bright, do not show it,
    And what if your tresses are gray?
If older, my heart does not know it;
    You live there, its bride-wife to-day.

The wedding-ring which you are wearing,
  Though thinner and seemingly old,
Shows nothing its value impairing,
  For that, like the wearer, is gold.

Though others have changed, I have never
  Seen change, nor its shadow, in you,
But, wayward though I, you have ever
  Been steadfast and constant and true.

And though fickle friends oft have wounded
  My heart, and abraded its faith,
Irrefut'ble proofs have abounded
  That you will be true until death.

And when such a treasure was given,
  It made life the sweeter to live;
What more could I ask of kind heaven?
  What more could kind heaven give?

But ere long we both shall be going
  To loved ones that people think dead,
To join—there is pleasure in knowing—
  Our Florence and Blannie and Fred.

Our winding-sheets now may be weaving,
  But, oh! 'twill be sweet when we start,
To know the dear ones we are leaving
  Are fondly united in heart.

They'll miss us,—perhaps miss us sadly,—
  But He who wipes tears from all eyes
Will guard them, and by and by, gladly,
  We'll welcome them all to the skies.

And sweet there will be the reunion,
  Beyond the cold, turbulent stream,
And blissful will be the communion,
  When vanishes earth like a dream.

And now, heaven grant us assistance
  In mind true to be, and in heart,
And soon to annihilate distance,
  That cruelly keeps us apart.

May tempest-clouds ne'er rise above you,
  To shadow and darken your skies,
May loving ones ne'er cease to love you,
  Nor sorrow bring tears to your eyes.

May joy and contentment be ever
  The stay and support of your heart,
And, true worth the test, they will never
  From that sweet asylum depart.

May life here be constantly bringing
  Its treasures for mind, heart, and soul,
To terminate only when, singing,
  You rise to the heavenly goal.

THE THREE GRACES.*

They stand like a triplet of beautiful birds,
    Suggestive of all that is charming in song,—
The harmony, music, and even the words,
    That strike and make captives the hearts of the throng;
And, like, too, those innocent birds, they suggest
    Whatever is peerless and lovely in thought,
The purest, the highest, the sweetest, the best
    That ever the visions of fancy have wrought.

They stand like a trio of roses in bloom,
    Their beauties imparting a halo around,
Dispersing all shadows and tinges of gloom,
    And causing with fragrance the air to abound;
And, like, too, those beautiful roses, they seem
    Suggestive of life's ever bright, sunny spring
And maidenhood's earliest, happiest dream,
    To which mem'ry ever and fondly will cling.

They stand like a grouping of stars, smiling down
    Serenely on earth from the heavenly height,
Their rays ever potent to conquer the frown,
    The gloom, and the deep, dismal darkness of night;
And, like, too, those sweet little stars, they impart
    A halo, transforming the night into day,—
A promise that strengthens and buoys up the heart,
    And banishes sombre forebodings away.

---

* On a picture of three young ladies standing before me.

They stand like a lovely, an angelic group,
  With soft, dimpled cheeks, rosy lips, and bright eyes,
As fair as the fairest of that countless troop
  That chant ceaseless anthems above the blue skies;
And, like, too, those fair, gentle angels above,
  Whose natures are by us all well understood,
They waken within us emotions of love,
  And cause us to worship the pure and the good.

Oh! sweet, gentle cousins, all peerlessly fair,
  If prayer of my soul can the heav'nly throne reach,
'Twill earnestly, lovingly breathe your names there,
  Invoking the richest of blessings on each.
May care never burden nor sorrow invade
  The hearts now all buoyant with hope and with love,
The roses upon your soft cheeks only fade
  To bloom still more sweetly forever above.

FICKLE FRIENDS.

Ah! I wonder, yes, I wonder,
  As I gaze on yon bright moon,
And reflect upon its changes,
  If the heart can change so soon;
I have watched the stars that glimmer
  But to fade at dawn of day,
And I wonder, yes, I wonder,
  Whether friendships fade as they.

I have seen the moon smile sweetly,
    And have seen a friend smile, too,
But anon these smiles have vanished
    From my eager, anxious view;
I have seen the bright stars flinging
    Floods of light from yonder sky,
Yet, when cloud-banks hung below them,
    They were hidden from the eye.

I have trusted friends, and loved them,
    And have thought that they loved me,
But too soon I've been awakened,
    My mistake, alas! to see;
I have seen these loved ones weary
    Of the now unpleasant ties,
And have seen, where erst was kindness,
    Cold indiff'rence in their eyes.

So I've o'er and often wondered,
    When I've made a calm review
Of life's many fickle changes,
    If the heart is ever true;
But I will not, cannot doubt it,
    Though the list of true be small,
For, though hosts of hearts are fickle,
    Yet it is not so with all.

But I wonder, still I wonder,
    Who among mankind to trust,
When my pure, sweet faith so often
    Has been scattered as the dust;

Comes to me the solemn answer,
  Like a voice from 'neath the sod,
" There is nothing true but heaven,"
  And no changeless friend but God.

ELMWOOD.

I WANDERED through Elmwood one calm autumn evening,
  The sunbeams played 'round me, and the breeze floated by;
The birds caroled softly, the silence relieving,
  And not a cloud-shadow could be seen in the sky.

The place and surroundings brought sad recollections
  Of a bright spring-time eve in this shady retreat;
And then, like a sunbeam, amid my reflections,
  Came one mem'ry o'er me that was rosy and sweet.

And yet, when reflecting on life and its changes,
  Its severed attachments, its joys and its woes,
How fate's stern decree heart from heart oft estranges,
  I envied the slumberers their dreamless repose.

For there, freed from trouble and sorrow, were sleeping
  The loved and the loving, who had long passed away,
No more sorrow knowing, nor sighing, nor weeping,—
  For Death's frigid fingers can all anguish allay.

Perhaps disappointed ambition there slumbers,—
  Some tongue, mute and silent, that was once wont to thrill
The eager, enchanted, and listening numbers,
  And sway them—as the tempest sways forests—at will.

Perhaps some sweet poet, whose harp is forever
  Unstrung, perchance broken, and a prey to the rust,
There dreamlessly slumbers, to awake again never
  Till the trump of the archangel wakens the dust.

Perhaps some fair maiden, whose lips oft had spoken
  Soft words that soothed sorrow and were potent to bless,
Found there 'neath the turf, when her sad heart was broken,
  Relief from all anguish and a balm for distress.

Ah! who can know ever how oft and unbidden
  The dark tears of sorrow have bedimmed brightest eyes,
Or how much of sadness and anguish are hidden
  By the green mound, all turf-grown, that heedlessly lies?

There are seasons of pleasure, seasons of gladness,
  When softly and brightly beams the soul through the eye,
There are seasons of sorrow, seasons of sadness,
  And then, 'twould be happiness, sweet solace, to die.

Ah me! life is cheerless, forlorn, dark, and dreary,
    When the sweet ties of friendship are broken in
        twain;
The heart becomes hopeless, despondent, and weary,
    And longs for the slumber whence 'twill ne'er wake
        again.

Sleep sweetly, ye loved ones, exempt from all trouble,
    I still 'mid its billows must awhile here abide,
Till when, like the bursting of glassy, bright bubble,
    "The golden bowl is broken," I sleep by your side.

BLIND.

FOR some wise purpose of His own—
    I seek not what it is, to know—
The God of Heaven, who has shown
    Kind care for mortals here below,
Has laid on me what others deem
    Affliction's load, which I must bear;
And yet, it does not heavy seem,
    I'm cheerful, though I cannot hear;
And if, sometimes, I should despond,
    And gloomy thoughts oppress my mind,
A monitor is near at hand,
    A cheerful, happy friend,—though blind!

Ah, yes! and I have often thought,
  When gazing in his sightless eyes,
That from his beaming smile I caught
  A glimpse of what, in yonder skies,
Gives glow and beauty to the scene,
  There, to immortal gaze unfurled,
Where all is peaceful and serene,
  And love illuminates a world—
A world where sweet contentment reigns—
  O'er sense and spirit, heart and mind,
And where a Saviour's love explains
  Why one was deaf, another blind.

And this young friend is but a youth,
  While I am in the yellow leaf,
His heart is warm with love and truth,
  And he is glad he is not deaf.
He does not murmur, does not pine;
  His youthful bosom heaves no sigh;
I think his burden more than mine,
  He thinks he's better off than I;
And when I see his beaming smile
  It seems like glimmer from above,
And in its light I read the while,
  His heart, his faith, his hope and love.

One morn, when all the earth was bright,
  Enrobed in gems of every hue,
And hearts were gladdened by the sight,
  Spread out in panoramic view,

I told my blind young friend that he
　Was subject for a poet's dream—
I *felt* that he was *more* to me—
　And would be some time, poet's theme;
I thought it then, and think it yet,
　And when he, smiling, asked me "why?"
I answered, and shall ne'er forget
　The wisdom of his calm reply.

Reminding him I could not hear,
　Perhaps a sad calamity,
Yet he had still a worse to bear,
　For he was blind and could not see.
"And still," I said, "you wear a smile,
　Seem always cheerful, calm and bright,
Though scenes that other hearts beguile
　Are darkly hidden from your sight."
He thus replied: "And why should I
　Be sad? It will not give me sight;
'Twill do no good to grieve or sigh,
　Who made me blind does only right."

My heart responded and I felt
　A lesson he had taught to me,
Who more than twice his years had dwelt
　'Mid beauties which he ne'er could see;
Yet oft, when I had seen some bird,
　With shining plumage, golden wing,
My mind by saddened thoughts was stirred,
　Because I could not hear him sing;

But never, since that morn, have come
    Such thoughts to rankle in my breast,
Sweet faith and hope have banished gloom
    And told me God knows what is best.

And though that calm and placid brow
    Is wrapped in dismal pall of night,
Within the bosom 'neath it, now,
    There is no gloom, for all is bright;
And though his eyes shall never glow,
    Like jewels in the sun's bright ray,
Yet he has shown, can ever show,
    Life's only peaceful, pleasant way;
And thoughtless men might wisely turn,
    Ere yet they reach their journey's end,
And calmly pause awhile to learn
    Life's lesson from my blind young friend.

A FRIEND'S A FRIEND FOR A' THAT.

To a true friend.

This world is all a changeful place,
    With truth and guile and a' that,
Where good with evil runs a race,
    Skies frown and smile and a' that.

For a' that and a' that,
　　Though storms portend and a' that,
If he is true,—and such as you,—
　　A friend's a friend for a' that.

When stern misfortune darkly comes,
　　The world's cold frown and a' that,
To bring distress upon our homes,
　　And weigh us down and a' that.
For a' that and a' that,
　　The wrath 'twill spend and a' that,
Our deepest woe will always show
　　A friend's a friend for a' that.

When wealth and luxuries abound,
　　And skies are bright and a' that,
A host of friends will gather round,
　　Attent, polite, and a' that.
For a' that and a' that,
　　What these pretend and a' that,
Pretence, we know, is tinsel show,
　　But friendship's pure for a' that.

The world is often harsh and rude
　　If we've not gold and a' that,
And meets us with repellent mood
　　And shoulders cold and a' that.
For a' that and a' that,
　　The ills that blend and a' that,
We need not weep if we can keep
　　One friend still true for a' that.

Mankind are selfish, we are told,
    And fickle, hard, and a' that;
Men worship rank and pow'r and gold,
    With high regard and a' that.
For a' that and a' that,
    Though knee they bend and a' that,
'Tis but a farce, where truth is scarce,
    True friends are gold for a' that.

WHEN I AM GONE.

When I am gone, and silent lie
Beyond the view of friendly eye,
Where words of love I may not hear,
Nor feel nor see affection's tear;
    Ah! I shall slumber sweetly then,
        For disappointment cannot come
    To lacerate my heart with pain,
        And o'er me fling a pall of gloom.

When I am gone, and calmly sleep
Beneath the turf, where willows weep,
Or where sweet roses bloom and fade,
And symbolize the slumb'ring dead,
    The withered leaves I shall not see,
        As storm-blasts strew them o'er the ground,
    And I shall all unconscious be
        Of coldness and distress around.

When I am gone, and dear ones who
To me have steadfast been and true,
Shall, with affection's tear-drops, lave
The mouldering sod upon my grave;
    Ah! I would then one moment wake
        To calm the sorrow in each breast,—
    A moment would death's silence break
        To tell them sweet is dreamless rest.

When I am gone, and cold my brow,
I happier far shall be than now;
Exempt from pain or doubt or dread,—
For these ne'er wake the sleeping dead,—
    I shall not feel misfortune's wave,
        Which hearts so oft with anguish fill,
    And though all lonely in my grave,
        There I shall slumber calmly still.

When I am gone, I would that those
Whom I shall cherish till life's close
Might sometimes kindly think of me,
Nor let me quite forgotten be;
    Yet, should remembrance waken pain,
        I'd have them banish me from thought;
    Unwept, unmourned, I would remain
        Recalled with love or else forgot.

EPITHALAMIUM.

Two stars shone smilingly above,
  Before fair Luna's throne,
Until by silken cords of love,
  The twain were bound in one;
Though brightly they had shone apart,
  Through every good and ill,
Yet, joined by tendrils of the heart,
  They shone more brightly still.

Like those two stars, down here were two,
  Drawn, like the twain above,
By cords resistless, strong and true,
  The same sweet cords of love;
And these, like those, though once apart
  Together sweetly came,
God having made them one in heart,
  Man made them one in name.

And sweetly may their young lives blend,
  And all its current flow
Serenely even to its end,
  Nor jar, nor ripple know;
And when the closing scene shall come,
  May they triumphant rise,
Up yonder to a blissful home,
  Together, in the skies.

THE STRICKEN HEART.

WHEN glides sad memory o'er the past,—
   Its sunshine and its clouds and storms,
Its buds and bloom by blight o'ercast,
   Its happy faces, graceful forms,—
Anon 'twill pause beside the grave,
   Or linger sadly o'er the bier,
Of hope which once sweet promise gave,
   Of bliss life's darkest gloom to cheer;
Then bravely it will strive to hide
   Its sorrow in the anguished breast,
And brushing bitter tears aside,
   'Twill in forgetfulness seek rest.

Ah! who can know what bitter pain
   Is often hid beneath a smile,
When come to memory's view again,
   The hopes that once could care beguile!
The hopes that gilded clouds with light,
   Drove all their dismal gloom away,
And luminated darkest night,
   With even "more than rapture's ray!"
To know that hopes so bright and sweet,
   That o'er life's sky such radiance shed,—
Now lie all blasted at our feet,
   Like withered flowers, cold and dead.

Bear up, ye faithful, stricken heart!
　The darkest night must pass away,
And all its dismal shades depart,
　Before the light of coming day;
Ay, though ye suffer, bleed and break,
　Bear up, for sorrow cannot last,
Be strong in faith and comfort take,
　In knowing all will soon be past;
For, oh! there is a healing balm,
　That can the deepest pain allay,
As after tempest comes a calm
　Whose smiles will drive all clouds away.

THE POET.

The poet's life, which all so rosy seems
　To others' eyes, so full of sweet delights,
So mixed with pleasing visions, joyous dreams,
　With happy valleys, and with flow'ry heights,
Is oft, alas! a slough of deep despond,
　A morn of toil and care, a sombre eve,
A night of rude unrest, with naught beyond
　That may or can the weariness relieve;

A night, indeed, of fitful, restless sleep,
　Succeeding to a day of murky gloom,
A stranded bark, o'er which wild billows sweep,
　A grief that solace finds but in the tomb;

Anon may come a glimm'ring ray of light
  To break the darkness that o'erspreads his sky,
And fling around a halo soft and bright,
  But even that will vanish by and by.

The poet's nature, aye, his heart and soul,
  Are all too sensitive, perhaps, to touch,
Too full of feeling which defies control,
  Too apt to brood o'er pains and sorrows much;
For *he* is not a poet, cannot be,
  Whose heart too cold and callous is to feel,
Whose eye can only life's plain roadway see,
  Heeds not his own, nor others', woe or weal.

They say 'tis genius, inspiration, art,
  A gift of nature, coveted and rare:
Nay, nay, 'tis none of these, 'tis but a heart,
  Alive to beauty, joy, or cold despair;
A heart that treasures friendship's sunny smiles,
  As heaven's dews that cause its flow'rs to bloom,
A heart too pure to dream of siren's wiles,
  A heart whose joys indiff'rence may entomb.

A poet is too little understood;
  He dwells in rosy bowers, or, perchance,
In isolated, gloomy solitude,
  Uncheered by one soft soul-inspiring glance;
Or if he haply finds a soul, anon,
  Congenial, and in nature like his own,
He yields to dreamy hope that he has won
  The friend long pined for, but, till now, unknown.

He trusts confidingly,—for so to trust
    His nature is,—and rears his temple high,
Till change and coldness crumble that to dust,
    And he is left o'er ruined hopes to sigh,
Too true himself to change as shifting breeze,
    Too trustful such a blow to apprehend,
He still hopes on, in faith, until he sees
    That change has come and life's sweet dream must end.

The poet's life is oft with sorrow blent,
    And though it may not always bring relief,
Yet when in song his hidden pain finds vent,
    It does calm down, and oft assuage, his grief;
His numbers calmly, like deep waters, flow,
    The fountain-head within his heart of hearts,
His suff'rings oft are like (as few can know)
    The pangs of deathless soul when hope departs.

And yet, with soul attuned to sweets of love,
    Harmonious, too, with joys that are divine,
A soul, that smile, or sigh, or tears can move,
    He may, and does, the purest thoughts enshrine;
And buoyed up by hope and love, his soulful flights
    Are as the eagle's o'er his eyrie home,
Anon he rises up to rapt'rous heights,
    And cleaves the misty blue of heaven's dome.

Ah! none can know, and time will ne'er reveal,
    The sweets of bliss, the anguish of despair,
The poet's pervious heart must often feel,—
    The joys it knows, the sorrows it must bear.

His song, conception does, perchance, convey,
  But still the more than half remains unsaid,
And this within his heart is hid away,
  To be with him entombed when he is dead.

VESPERS (ST. PETER'S, MEMPHIS).

Up yonder beams the moon, revealing
  A world of gems earth ne'er can know;
Down here the vespers, softly stealing,
  "Praise God from whom all blessings flow,"
While worshippers, devoutly kneeling,
  The beauty of devotion show.

Up, now, from earnest souls are welling
  The praises of the God above,
While sacred anthems, softly swelling,
  Fill every arch and each alcove,
All evil, carnal thoughts dispelling,
  And filling every soul with love.

Now softly on the night-breeze trilling,
  And all in harmony complete,
These grand old walls with music filling
  Float melodies all grand and sweet,
The turbulence of nature stilling,
  And all with holy love replete.

Oh! while these strains are round me ringing
    And floating on the balmy air,
I fancy seraphs here are singing
    The songs of some celestial sphere;
And I, too, humble spirit bringing,
    Bow head and heart in praise and prayer.

OH! ASK ME NOT TO SING TO-NIGHT.

Song.

Oh! ask me not to sing to-night,—
    My song would sad reflections bring;
Oh! ask me not to sing to-night,
    For I am sad and cannot sing.
The heart is often wrung with pain
    When cold and calm the eye appears,
And strives—but oft, alas! in vain—
    To hide from view its surging tears.

Oh! ask me not to sing to-night
    Amid the gay and joyous throng,
'Twould chill at once their hearts' delight
    To hear my sad and mournful song.
The wounded heart would not betray
    Its woes in saddened notes and sighs,—
No; let it hide them all away
    From careless and unfeeling eyes.

Oh! ask me not to sing to-night,
    For hapless mem'ries rise to view
That put all joyousness to flight,
    And make me sad and silent, too.
I loved, I worshipped, and my sky
    With radiant beams was overspread,
Nor did I think that hope could die,
    But now, alas! 'tis cold and dead.

Oh! ask me not to sing to-night,
    When all the world is dark to me;
You want a joyous song and light,
    And mine would sad and mournful be;
'Twould in no heart an echo wake,
    You'd hear it only to condemn,
For I alone could silence break
    To sing my dead hope's requiem.

YOU SANG "THAT SONG" FOR ME TO-NIGHT.

You sang that song for me to-night;
    It called to mind a fadeless dream
Of when, one autumn evening bright,
    I heard it on the flowing stream.
Its echoes long have silent been,
    And she who sang is far away,
But your sweet song brought back the scene,
    Which can from mem'ry ne'er decay.

You sang that song for me to-night;
　Its melodies are ling'ring yet,
And sweet reflections they incite,
　And sad ones, too, which I'd forget.
A song will sometimes call to mind
　A scene of pleasure, yet, again,
Its sweetest notes anon will find
　Their echoes in some hidden pain.

You sang that song for me to-night,
　And though 'twas rich in melody,
And sweet to those whose hearts were light,
　'Twas sad as it was sweet to me;
And while its notes all sweetly rang,
　Like those of some melodious bird,
My heart connected, while you sang,
　A memory with every word.

You sang that song for me to-night,
　And mem'ry still recalls each tone,
As here, beneath the moon's pale light,
　I sit in silence, all alone.
I gaze upon the jewelled sky,
　The moon, and stars that round her play;
I hear soft zephyrs murm'ring by,
　And think of loved ones far away.

You sang that song for me to-night,
　And while my soul drank every sound,
It in each trill and tone and flight
　A melancholy pleasure found.

Yet there are wounds time does not heal,
And pains that it can ne'er allay,
But sing again, and I shall feel
There is for me a brighter day.

DROP BY DROP.

Drop by drop the water trickles
　On the rocks that heedless lie
Yet these rocks will show the power
　Of those drippings by and by.
Although angry waves defying,
　And by tempest's wrath unharmed,
Though by lightning blast unshaken,
　Unabashed, and unalarmed,
Yet to soothing touch how yielding
　As it softly, day by day,
Comes to smooth with gentle fingers
　Rough uncouthness all away.

So the human heart, though hardened,
　Like the firm, unshaken rock,
And with iron nerve resisting
　Stern misfortune's rudest shock,
Foes defying, threat'nings scorning,
　Rudeness meeting with its kind,
Taunts with harsher taunts returning,
　Ne'er to wrong or ill resigned;

Yet a sympathetic tear-drop
　Will its deep foundations move,
And it opens, yields, and softens
　To the gentle voice of love.

Let us learn from this a lesson—
　Long too little understood—
That each heart contains a fountain,
　Somewhere in it hid, of good,
And that stones will only choke it,
　Stop its soft and cheering flow,
Rough, harsh treatment may destroy it,
　And produce a gulf of woe;
But, if it be cared for kindly,
　Like the gold without alloy,
It will bear all tests and trials,
　And will prove a fount of joy.

"DUM SPIRO, SPERO."

We've said farewell, but not forever,
　Faith and hope have whispered this,
Nor dare I think that I shall never
　Realize my dream of bliss.
It may be madness thus to cherish
　Hopes that ne'er to fruit may grow,
Hopes that soon, alas, may perish
　Like the roses 'neath the snow;

But there is a present gladness—
Which can soothe the deepest pain,
Soften sorrow, sweeten sadness—
In the thought they are not vain.

Is it madness thus to love thee,
Thus to worship at thy shrine,
And hope that love will move thee
Yet, to tell me thou art mine?
These sweet words thou ne'er hast spoken,
And perhaps wilt never speak,
But hast thou no promise broken?
And wilt thou no promise break?
Nay, dear one, I will not doubt thee,
For thy heart is free from guile,
And though I must live without thee,
Let me live in hope the while.

Vain may be the aspiration
Thee to claim as all mine own,
Yet I give thee adoration
Such as woman ne'er has known;
And though scores may kneel before thee,
Offering their love for thine,
Other heart can ne'er adore thee
As thou art adored by mine.
This perchance thou mayst remember,
Back 'twill come on mem'ry's wave,
When the snows of cold December
Lie upon my lonely grave.

But I'll still indulge in dreaming
    That my hopes are not in vain,
And that skies, though sombre seeming,
    May be bright o'er me again,—
Brighter even than when wearing
    Softest tints that float above,
While my eager heart was hearing
    From thy lips sweet words of love.
Dearest! soften separation;
    All I ask of thee is this:
Promise me realization
    Of my one sweet dream of bliss.

"DO COTTON PAY?"

The question was up in the "Deestrict Five Club"
"Do cotton pay farmers?" Ah! there was the rub.
Discuss it they did, as they ploughed, scraped, and hoed,
In town, at the shop, in the fields, on the road,
On highways and by-ways, on horseback and train,
In snow and in sunshine, in wind and in rain,
At church in the morning ere "meetin'" begun,
And then, again, too, when the "preachin'" was done,
And even sometimes when they knelt down to pray
The question obtruded, "Do cotton pay?"

The club met on Friday, threw open the door,
And old Farmer Martin, all knew, had the floor,

For he'd been "app'inted" to make 'em a speech,
And every one knew that good sense he would teach;
So crowds had collected, quite eager, that day
To hear words of wisdom on "Do cotton pay?"

"To order!" was called,—Farmer Diggs in the chair;
He stroked down his whiskers and brushed back his hair,
The question announced, then leaned back in his seat
As old Farmer Martin rose up to his feet,
Took out his huge quid, and, observing 'twas new,
With care wrapped it up till the speaking was through;
Then, clearing his throttle, he straightway began,
And I will report him as well as I can.

SPEECH OF FARMER MARTIN BEFORE "DEES-TRICT FIVE CLUB," COTTON COUNTY, MISSISSIPPI.

Do cotton pay? is what you want to know.
I've follered it fur forty year or mo',
An' some er you hev follered it as long;
We thought it payed, but mebbe we was wrong.
Now let us see. Well, brother farmers, I
Have worked it hard, an' sold it low an' high,
Pinched close, an' saved at all the corners, yet,
When Christmas come, I found myself in debt;
But on I went, an' planted, ploughed, an' hoed,
In hopes o' payin' all the debts I owed
An' havin' somethin' left to put away
Fur (what I knowed would come) a rainy day.

In May an' June I've plodded through my fields,
Felt mighty happy in ther promised yields,
An' thought I'd never seen so fine a crap,
An' didn't have no fears o' no mishap,
Tell bymeby, as I walked along the lane,
Jest thinkin' how I'd like to see it rain,
I see the blooms, an' here an' yon the forms,
An' then I see the plaguey little worms,
An' in the bottom see the signs o' rust,
An' 'twixt the two I don't know which is wust.

I mighty quick concluded in my mind
My whole year's work 'ud leave me still behind;
I'd counted on "a bale,"—ur little less—
(But cotton's somethin' 'bout which 'twon't do to
　　guess),
An' when 'twas picked and ginned, my sakes alive!
Instead of one to one, 'twas one to five!
A half a bale some farmers said they'd made;
I knowed I hadn't, an' it nuver paid,—
Leastways, it didn't pay that year I know,
Yet I was kept the year-long on the go.

One year I planted corn an' oats an' wheat,
An' tried to raise a smoke-house full o' meat;
Jest planted cotton so's to keep in seeds,
An' ploughed an' hoed to keep down grass an' weeds.
That season was the best I ever had,
An', like a fool, I got "rip snortin'" mad;
I cussed things blue; yes, brothers, cussed an' swore,
Jest let right loose, like wild, and ripped and tore.

My cotton was the best I ever made,
An' ef I'd planted more it would er paid.
I seed it all, but then it was too late,
And so I cussed at my bad luck or fate;
But I'm not all as shows their want o' sense
By doin' wrong then blamin' Providence.

Well, as I said, I'd but a little patch,
An' out o' that could no big money hatch;
An' so I sobered down, an' 'twas not long
Afore I see how fur I'd stumbled wrong,
An' ef I'd planted more, 'twas likely I
'Der paid my debts an' laid a little by,
Fur prices that year kept on goin' up,
An' didn't seem to pint to wher they'd stop.
But, after all, I reckon I'd er sold
Afore the rise,—in debt how could I hold?—
An' then agin, though I had plenty pluck,
To sell too soon had always been my luck.
The intrust I was payin' then was steep,
An' craps an' lands was mortgaged in a heap.

I tell you, brother farmers, an' 'tis true,
This thing o' mortgagin' and sich won't do;
You've sometimes signed away yer craps, an' found
'Em sold an' gone afore put in the ground.
You talk about the farmer's swettin' brow,
But I can tell you, though you know it now,
The man who mortgages from year to year
Is more a slave than ever niggers were.

His lands, his teams, his craps, an' everything
That will a dollar or a nickel bring
Is chained an' locked, and bymeby he will see
The money-lender grips an' holds the key.
But, as I said before, one year I tried
Grain crap an' hogs, an' let King Cotton slide.
Besides all these I had an' run a mill,
Sawed lumber—but I didn't run a still.

My corn did well, my oats not much, my wheat
Made little more than I an' mine could eat;
My mill was often stopped for want of logs,
While chol'ra an' the niggers got my hogs,—
Leastways not every one; they left a few,
An' fur my fam'ly meat these had to do.
So thar I was, owin' debts I couldn't pay;
I tell you I was blue *as blue* that day,
When countin' up an' findin' to my cost
That all my hard licks of the year was lost.
An' then I tried to work the question out,
Do cotton pay? Concluded that it mout,
An' then, agin, it moutn't, but that I
Could not afford experiments to try,
But still would plant an' plough an' hoe an' pick,
An', like a June bug, to King Cotton stick;
Fur farmers can't afford to stand stock still,
Ef cotton don't pay, tell they find what will.

We've got to work ef we would eat an' live,
An' doctors rarely take the pills they give;

They physic us an' tell us what to do,
But seldom they what they advise pursue.
Let them as knows so much about the craps
Show something that will pay; then we, perhaps,
Will take a hand, especially ef they,
By working at it, show us that 'twill pay.
'Tis my opinion them as talks don't know,
An' if they'll try ther plans ten years or so
They'll more than we uv money feel the lack,
An' find it safe to keep the beaten track;
Leastways, I'll say—of this there is no doubt—
'Tis best to raise what you know most about,
Pervidin', always, climate and the sile
Ar' suited to it; then, though small the pile
That you may lay aside, 'tis certain, sure,
An' nothin' would have made it any more.

Them Yankee fellers who, some years ago,
Perfessed so much 'bout farmers' work to know,
An' come down here to wonders work an' sich,
An', in no time, to get big money rich,
Remained awhile, an' flourished 'round, an' then
They went back poorer, but much wiser, men;
An' though 'tis certain they no money made,
Perhaps, to them—in larnin'—cotton paid. .
Ef I was somewhere else, perhaps I mout
Examine operations round about,
An' then the plan, I think, that I'd pursue,
Would be to do as I see others do.

But cotton pays some folks, and *that* we know,
For many people rich upon it grow,

An' speculators lots o' money make,
Though now and then a whole lot of 'em break;
But, after all, each takes his chance, an' all,
Like us, are liable to rise an' fall,
An' spite of speculators an' what not,
We're safe ef we can hold what we have got.
"Do cotton pay?" I think we'd better stand
At what we're at; improve our worn-out land,
Make every acre richer than before,
An' make it bring each year a little more.

Raise plenty corn, pertaters, oats, an' wheat,
An' always try to raise a plenty meat;
Keep out o' debt, let mortgages alone,
E'en ef you hunger an' must gnaw a bone;
Fur better that than have crap, house, an' lands
All go into the money-lender's hands,—
Fur, as I said afore, yer mortgagee
Holds you more slave than niggers ever be.
When mortgages is wanted get away,
An' mebbe you'll larn bymeby that cotton'll pay.
Stick to yer work an' put yer best licks thar,
An' ef comes bad years, don't you then despar,
But work right on, an' I'll tell you, "sure pop,"
That soon or later you'll come out a-top.

CANTATRIX DULCISSIMA.

(Miss Emma Abbott.)

WHEN winter-blasts are cold and bitter,
    And winter clouds drop freezing rains,
And streamlets in the sunlight glitter,
    All bound and still in icy chains,
Fair nature pines in jewelled sadness,
    And longs for balmy, rosy spring,
When grove and glen resound with gladness,
    While birds their tuneful anthems sing.

So, when the heart is bowed in sorrow,
    And burdened with a load of care,
It pines and longs relief to borrow
    From pain and grief and cold despair;
It looks beyond the gloom surrounding,
    And listens for the soothing voice
Of music, on the air resounding,—
    For music makes the heart rejoice.

Ah, yes! sweet music conquers sadness;
    It gives the troubled soul relief,
Into it pours a stream of gladness,
    Which brings forgetfulness of grief;

For woes that force the scalding tear,
    For every sorrow, every ill,
It is a potent panacea,
    The sweetest nature could distill.

Thus, lady, when the heart is laden,
    Thy song dispels the gloom of night,
The soul enwraps in dreams of Aidenn,
    And fills it with celestial light.
Oh, sweetest singer! mayst thou never
    A sorrow know nor feel a care,
May happiness be thine forever,
    Both here on earth and then *up there!*

HONOR.

'Tis life, 'tis more,
    Ah, yes! far more,
For life is death without it;
    And high-souled man
    Feels naught more than
Have friends or foes to doubt it.

If he be poor,
    He feels this more
Than were fair fortune smiling
    With favors rare,
    To banish care,
His troubles all beguiling.

No heavier blow
The heart can know,
Whatever hopes it cherished,
Than hear the loved
Say aught has proved
Its honor all has perished.

And if the steel
Which he must feel
Thus, by loved hand is driven,
'Twill pierce the heart
To vital part,
And fatal blow is given.

The wound is deep,
'Twere vain to weep,
For tears will but reveal it;
It rankles there,
And breeds despair,
And death alone can heal it.

"HOMEWARD NOW THE SWALLOWS FLY."

(School-girls returned home.)

HOMEWARD now the school-girls come,
　Each one wears a happy smile,
Glad again to be at home,
　Glad to rest from books awhile;

Loved companions they have left,
    Scenes and friends and places dear,
Yet they do not feel bereft,
    Dearer ones have met them here.

Proofs abundant, too, they bring
    That of time they made no waste,
But through winter months and spring
    Idle hours they rarely passed;
Like the bees that from the flow'rs
    Gather honey while they may,
They improved life's sunny hours,
    And have treasures stored away.

O'er them hang soft, dreamy skies,
    Round them cluster kindred dear,
Bright the scenes that greet their eyes,
    Sweet the words of love they hear;
And if now and then perchance
    Backward they, amid their glee,
Turn a retrospective glance,
    Pleasing scenes alone they see.

Happy girlhood! rosy now,
    Blossoms all its way adorn;
Oh! may never shadowed brow
    Tell of cruel, hidden thorn;
Flowers blooming all around,
    Fragrance on the breezes fling;
May those sweets through life abound,
    Peace and joy alone to bring.

But the school-girls now at home
    Must not fancy life a dream;
Cares, and trials too, will come,—
    All things are not what they seem,—
Morning brings us cheering light,
    But 'twill ere long pass away,
For the shades of sombre night
    Never fail to follow day.

This the young should ne'er forget;
    Then, when backward glance they cast,
Naught to waken vain regret
    They will see in all the past;
Smiling faces let them wear,
    Hearts to cheer and lighten homes,
But they, too, must learn to bear
    Disappointment when it comes.

May they sorrow never know,
    Heaven ever on them smile,
Richest gifts on them bestow,
    And preserve their hearts from guile;
May indeed life be a dream
    Sweet to them, and when 'tis past,
May they find beyond death's stream
    Blissful homes in heav'n at last.

SHE'S SWEETEST WHEN SHE SMILES.

With bright brown eyes and auburn hair,
    With cherry lips and rosy cheeks,
A gentle and bewitching air,
    A voice of music when she speaks,
With smile that has the sunlight caught,—
    Adept though in coquettish wiles,—
Oh, she is lovely! and I've thought
    That she is sweetest when she smiles.

And then I've sat and gazed again,—
    And I could gaze till I were blind,—
She seemed in meditative vein,
    And as I gazed I changed my mind;
I gazed on lips and eyes and head,
    A soft subdued, calm shadow had
O'erspread her features, and I said,
    "No, she is sweetest when she's sad."

Another time I saw her, when
    A cloud swept swiftly o'er her brow;
My eyes were transfixed on her then,
    And "Oh!" I thought, "she's lovely now."
Not Scotland's queen to anger wrought,
    Nor all earth's queens with dazzling crowns
Were half so lovely, and I thought,
    "Oh! she is sweetest when she frowns."

I looked again, and there she stood,
   Her own resplendent lovely self,
In beauty of young womanhood,
   And witching as a fairy elf;
Like lily sparkling in the dew,
   Surpassing flow'rs of every clime,
She seemed, and as I gazed I knew
   She's sweet and lovely all the time.

THOSE EYES OF HEAVENLY BLUE.

(Dedicated to their owner.)

Those eyes, those eyes of azure hue,
   So sweetly, so serenely bright,—
Those eyes of purest heav'nly blue,
   That gleam with softest sweetest light;
They seem to flash like jewels rare,
   No brighter in Golconda's mine,
And not a gem that glitters there
   Can shed a lustre more divine.

With moving light I see them blaze,
   Yet calm they seem to be and meek,
And when into their depths I gaze
   I almost fancy that they speak.

I wonder if a calm, soft eye,
    Of dimless, fadeless, heav'nly blue,
Fails ever here to typify
    The changeless, constant, and the true.

Ah! I have looked on eyes that seemed
    A wealth of softness to reveal,
And later found they only beamed
    O'er hearts as cold and hard as steel;
With warmth of love they seemed to glow,
    And with a liquid light to beam,
And yet I learned from them to know
    Things are not always what they seem.

I love an eye that feeling shows,
    And that a tender softness wears,
An eye in which true love-light glows,
    And sweeter seems in sparkling tears.
But those of artful, vain coquette,
    Who lives and cares for self alone,
With pearly tears are never wet,—
    True feeling is to her unknown.

The blue, the soft, bewitching blue,
    That gives its tint to beauty's eye,
The pure, the constant, and the true
    Was meant alone to typify;
But sometimes, like the fickle ray
    That flickers o'er the marsh at night,
And lures the trav'ler from his way,
    It sheds a false and treach'rous light.

But those which have my muse inspired,
　And caused my grov'lling thoughts to soar,
Too bright to merely be admired,
　Are such as truest men adore,
Are such as hardest hearts would heed,
　And to their glances yield control:
They azure windows are, indeed,
　Through which is seen a peerless soul.

BIRTH OF A FLOWER.

(Tribute to a young Canadian lady friend; written on her birthday.)

THE sweetest flowers bloom in spring,
　When skies are soft, serene, and fair,
And then it is they freely fling
　The soothing fragrance on the air;
Then, too, the happy birds of song
　Are heard among the leafy trees,
When, from their perches, all day long
　They freight with music every breeze.

The moon, on her cerulean throne,
　Seems fairer, calmer, brighter then,
And down upon this lower zone
　Sends softer rays through grove and glen;
And all the smiling stars above
　That round about her court we see,
Evincing reverence and love,
　Seem then more beautiful to be.

The earth, which erewhile seemed so sad,
　So bleak and barren, cold and drear,
Is then in velvet verdure clad,
　And seems a joyous smile to wear,
While zephyrs, laden with perfume,
　Like angel-breathings glide along,
Dispel all sombre shades of gloom,
　And seem to murmur notes of song.

And spring, arrayed in beauty's gear,
　That bears no tinsel touch of art,
Sweet spring, of all the changeful year,
　Is dearest to the "pure in heart."
How fitting, then, that such a time,
　When gladness reigned supreme in power,
The fates should bless you icy clime,
　By giving it a lovely flower!

A flower that, despite the snow
　And ice that later wrapped its home,
Should still more fair and lovely grow,
　And winter, as in spring-time, bloom;
A flower that, I know, was made
　To some sweet destiny fulfill;
A flower that can never fade,
　But will for aye bloom sweetly still.

This flower, lady, wears thy form,
　Sees through thy beauteous, bright brown eyes,
Enwraps a heart sincere and warm,
　And smiles as bright as sunny skies.

A tropical I know 'tis not,
    For, in the far up north it came;
I cannot designate the spot,
    But know that "Emma" is its name.

Perennially may it bloom,
    As now be ever fair and bright,
Its sweetness banish care and gloom,
    And yield to loving hearts delight;
For well I know if it but give
    To others what of joy it can,
'Twill happy be, itself, to live,
    However long may be life's span.

It came, as I have said, in spring,
    When winter's reign had passed away;
It came a world of joy to bring,
    And this is its bright natal day;
A day to be remembered long,
    Till love's pure fires shall cease to burn,
And many a dear and loving throng
    Will hail with gladness its return.

Let me with other friends unite,
    Fair lady, on this lovely morn,
In hailing with sincere delight
    The day on which this flower was born;
And let me, too, with them express,
    Though better far will they than I,
The wish that heav'n may ever bless
    Its life, in time and "by and by."

"Sometime," I know, its bright brown eyes
    Will close on earthly scenes for aye,
May then they sparkle in the skies,
    In spring-time's bright perpetual day;
And in that purer world above,
    Where skies are ever soft and fair,
And every breeze is sweet with love,
    Oh, may it bloom forever there!

HOME.

(To a friend.)

Home, with all its world of treasures,
    Loving words and sunny smiles,
Cheering and substantial pleasures,
    Where no vice the Lares defiles;
Home, where all the daily greetings
    Are with fond devotion blest;
Home, where tender, loving meetings
    Sanctify and sweeten rest.

Home, where sunlight, ever beaming,
    Spreads a halo all around;
Home, where love, when sweetly dreaming,
    Hears no harsh discordant sound;

Home, where loving father, mother,
  Watch their darling ones at play,
All devoted to each other,
  Happy as the length of day.

Home, where pleasing recreations
  No contentions e'er despoil;
Home, whose ties and sweet relations
  Amply compensate for toil;
Home, where patt'ring footsteps meet you,
  Fall like music on your ear;
Home, where childish kisses greet you,
  While maturer ones wait near.

Home, where order, comfort, neatness,
  Meet the eye at every glance,
All in beautiful completeness,
  Which no labor may enhance;
Home like this, my friend, possessing,
  Sweet content your heart should fill,
Earth could give no higher blessing
  Than you have at Terrace Hill.

There—where ofttimes I have found you,
  And your happiness could see—
With your loved ones all around you,
  May you ever happy be.
I—and possibly misguided—
  Followed fate till I am here,
From my loved ones far divided,
  Vainly wishing they were near.

Yet I envy not my neighbor,—
   No, this folly mine is not,—
Envy could not lighten labor,
   Nor make pleasanter my lot;
In your home-life may you ever
   Be, my friend, supremely blest;
I'll go on, forgetting never
   That " whatever is is best."

AROUND THE HEARTHSTONE.

(December 24, 1883.)

Around the hearthstone, happy, smiling,
   Sit my loved ones, all save one,
The hour of Christmas-eve beguiling,
   As before we oft have done;
The hour for pleasing converse only,
   Not for meditative mood,
The hours till now to me so lonely,
   In my cheerless solitude.

The fire is blazing dimly, slowly,
   Wintry winds have ceased to blow,
The warm clouds hang above us lowly,
   Yet no threat'ning outlines show;
The air seems more like calm September,
   Or like balmy, flow'ry May,
Than like to bleak and cold December;
   More like spring than winter day.

And daylight has but just departed,
    Shades of night are gath'ring near,
Alone to find a happy-hearted,
    Loving, cheerful circle here;
The younger ones their joy displaying,
    As the young can do alone,
The "gude wife" busily crocheting,
    All around the old hearthstone.

Oh! sweet to me to be surrounded
    Thus by loved ones here once more,
Where erst the sturdy walls resounded
    With love's notes in days of yore;
Around the hearthstone, happy, smiling,
    Children gathering in their glee,
Allaying sorrow, care beguiling,
    Bringing only joy to me.

How happy he, 'mid wintry weather,
    When the snow-flakes carpets weave,
Who can, around his hearthstone, gather
    All his loved ones Christmas-eve;
And sweet the thought, with fond hope blended,—
    As will love and hope e'er blend,—
That when these gath'rings here have ended,
    There'll be one that shall not end.

SONG.

Alas! thou hast cruelly wounded
    The heart whose devotion was thine,
The death-knell of hope thou hast sounded,
    And now not a glimmer is mine.
Thou leavest me lonely and saddened,
    My heart is all aching with pain,—
That heart which thy smile oft has gladdened,
    But never may gladden again.

Alas! though to me thou hast spoken
    The words thou wilt never forget;
Yet ties thou hast ruthlessly broken,
    Which formed when we long ago met.
Our spirits, I thought, were congenial,
    For up in our bosoms love sprung;
I hoped 'twould continue perennial,
    But mine, now, away thou hast flung.

Alas! from my sweet dream I waken
    To find a cloud over me spread;
That I am condemned and forsaken,
    And life's sweetest hopes are all dead.
Thou hast cruelly, bitterly wounded
    The heart that was wholly thine own;
The knell of its hopes thou hast sounded,
    And hopeless I'm left and alone.

www.ingramcontent.com/pod-product-compliance
Lightning Source LLC
Chambersburg PA
CBHW021825230426
43669CB00008B/866